MW01044723

Learning First,
Technology Second

*The Educator's Guide
to Designing Authentic Lessons*

Liz Kolb

International Society for Technology in Education
PORTLAND, OREGON • ARLINGTON, VA

Learning First, Technology Second
The Educator's Guide to Designing Authentic Lessons
By Liz Kolb

© 2017 International Society for Technology in Education
World rights reserved. No part of this book may be reproduced or transmitted in any form or by any means—electronic, mechanical, photocopying, recording, or by any information storage or retrieval system—without prior written permission from the publisher. Contact Permissions Editor: iste.org/about/permissions-and-reprints; permissions@iste.org; fax: 1.541.302.3780.

Editor: *Valerie Witte*
Copy Editor: *Steffi Drewes*
Proofreader: *Kristin Ferraioli*
Indexer: *Wendy Alex*
Cover Design: *Edwin Ouellette*
Book Design and Production: *Kim McGovern*

Library of Congress Cataloging-in-Publication Data

Names: Kolb, Liz, author.
Title: Learning first, technology second : the educator's guide to designing authentic lessons / By Liz Kolb.
Description: Portland, Oregon : International Society for Technology in Education, [2017] | Includes bibliographical references and index.
Identifiers: LCCN 2016059616 (print) | LCCN 2017003566 (ebook) | ISBN 9781564843890 (pbk.) | ISBN 9781564846310 (mobi) | ISBN 9781564846327 (epub) | ISBN 9781564846334 (pdf)
Subjects: LCSH: Educational technology. | Education—Effect of technological innovations on. | Lesson planning.
Classification: LCC LB1028.3.K649 2017 (print) | LCC LB1028.3 (ebook) | DDC 371.33—dc23
LC record available at https://lccn.loc.gov/2016059616

First Edition
ISBN: 9781564843890
Ebook version available

Printed in the United States of America

ISTE® is a registered trademark of the International Society for Technology in Education.

About ISTE

The International Society for Technology in Education (ISTE) is the premier nonprofit organization serving educators and education leaders committed to empowering connected learners in a connected world. ISTE serves more than 100,000 education stakeholders throughout the world.

ISTE's innovative offerings include the ISTE Conference & Expo, one of the biggest, most comprehensive ed tech events in the world—as well as the widely adopted ISTE Standards for learning, teaching and leading in the digital age and a robust suite of professional learning resources, including webinars, online courses, consulting services for schools and districts, books, and peer-reviewed journals and publications. Visit iste.org to learn more.

About the Author

Liz Kolb is a clinical assistant professor at the University of Michigan in Ann Arbor where she teaches courses in education technology to preservice teachers. She is the author of several books, including *Cell Phones in the Classroom: A Practical Guide for the K–12 Educator* (ISTE 2011) and *Help Your Child Learn with Cell Phones and Web 2.0* (ISTE 2013). In addition, Liz has published numerous articles and book chapters on new technologies and education in prominent publications, such as *Education Leadership, Scholastic,* Edutopia, ISTE's Edtekhub, and *Learning and Leading with Technology.*

Liz has done consulting work and has been a featured and keynote speaker at conferences all over the United States and Canada. Liz co-developed the annual 4T Virtual Conference in 2011 and runs the blog cellphonesinlearning.com. She is also the creator of the Triple E Framework for effective teaching with digital technologies. Liz is a former social studies and computer technology teacher. Liz currently resides in Ann Arbor, Michigan.

Acknowledgments

The Triple E Framework, research, and case studies presented in this book come from a collaboration of many master teachers and thought leaders in education technology. I do not have room enough here to show my gratitude for their contributions, but I do want to name a few of the many who were particularly helpful with this book and the Framework behind it. Thanks to the following educators for sharing their inspiring lessons for this book: Tammy Church, Evelyn Daugherty, Kyle Dunbar, Kelly Grahl, Todd Hausman, Adam Hellebuyck, Rory Hughes, Alyssa Marcangelo, Stephanie Passman, Jeff Stanzler, Booke Stidham, and Tom Ward. I am standing on the shoulders of many educational leaders, without whom the Triple E Framework would not have been possible. This includes (but is not limited to) the creators of the TPACK, SAMR, and TIM (as well as many other models for technology integration). There are numerous teachers and school districts in Michigan, Indiana, Illinois, and Wisconsin that were willing to try the Framework, long before we knew it worked well, and I thank them for taking a risk and giving me the necessary feedback to improve the model. Most specifically, I am grateful to Melissa Brooks-Yip, Delia DeCourcy, Kristin Fontichiaro, Teresa McMahon, Kevin Upton, Jeff Stanzler, and Amber White for their professional collaboration and willingness to volunteer their time to a conference based on many of the ideas and research shared in this book. My fellow Michigan Association for Computer Users in Learning (MACUL) Board members who have helped me grow as an educator and inspire me to think differently about research and practice. My colleagues at the University of Michigan, in particular my mentor Barry Fishman, who always believed in me and often reminds me that there is no snake oil in education technology (a phrase I love to borrow). Many other colleagues have also supported my work, including (but again, not limited to): Deborah Ball, Tim Boerst, Ellen Byerlin, Maria Coolican, Betsy Davis, Joanna Elliot, Kendra Hearn, Debi Khasnabis, Elizabeth Moje, Pete Pasque, Chris Quintana, Cathy Reischl, Katie Robertson, Shari Saunders, Elliot Soloway, Annemarie Sullivan Palincsar, and Meri Tenney Murihead. Most importantly, my current and former students inspire and challenge me each and every day to be a better teacher and learner.

I am grateful to ISTE for their continued support of my work and their efforts to continuously improve the work of technology in education—in particular Emily Reed, who helped start the conversation for publishing this book, and Valerie Witte, who had the unenviable task of editing my writing and ultimately making this into a lovely work of art. It has been a pleasure and thrill to work so closely with these experts.

Dedication

For Brent, Meghan, and Sam, without whom this book would have been completed a few years earlier, but there would be nobody to celebrate it with. I prefer the long wait and celebration. I am happy for each of you.

Contents

Introduction

Designing Lessons for Authentic Engagement

AS A TEACHER EDUCATOR, I frequently ask new and veteran teachers why they use technology. One of the most common answers I hear is that technology engages students. This emphasis on engagement in learning through technology is not only coming from practitioners. Research on technology in education repeatedly focuses on how technology can engage or excite students during a lesson. For example, when school leaders were asked the benefits for using technology in learning in a recent survey by Project Tomorrow (2016), the number one reason given was that the technology increased student engagement in school. There are numerous studies citing that technology contributed to student engagement (Bebell & O'Dwyer, 2010; Martinez & Schilling, 2011; Spires et al., 2008). Many of these studies leave the impression that simply using a digital device is magical motivation for students, moving them from noninvolvement in class activities to active engagement. While this is useful research, in my 20 years of teaching, I have found that technology almost always engages students. However, over the last six years, I have come to understand that there are different types of engagement when it comes to technology tools. Authentic engagement is not about using a specific technology tool; rather it puts the learning outcomes first and the technology choices second. This book shares what authentic engagement looks like, sounds like, and feels like in learning. The framework introduced in this book, the Triple E, will allow teachers to put the needs of the learner first, and then select the technology tools that leverage authentic engagement in the instructional goals.

The Pitfalls of False Engagement

Many studies measure engagement through observation—in other words, if students are observed looking at learning software or using a digital device, they are labeled "engaged." Yet, just because a child is swiping through an iPad does not necessarily mean he or she is focused on the process of learning; the child could easily be swiping quickly to get to the fun game at the end and not actually comprehending the content. This is *false* or *flawed engagement,* the observational assumption that because a student is actively using a technology tool, he or she is engaged in learning, when, in reality, the student may not be meeting the desired learning goals. An example of false engagement would be a teacher using a web-based tool to give a mobile quiz and a student answering the questions via cell phone, but focusing on being the first one to answer rather than understanding the nature and purpose of the questions. Engagement in learning goals is different than engagement in using a tool or website. Thus, buyer beware: engagement through access alone can quickly become a gimmick, so be wary of only using technology because it will engage students in a device or screen.

Allow me to elaborate with my own story of false engagement. When I began teaching in 1996, I learned how to use PowerPoint. In the 1990s, knowing how to use PowerPoint was rare for a classroom teacher. I was so taken with the "fun" of the tool that I decided to experiment and turn one of my traditional overhead projector lectures into a PowerPoint presentation. Immediately, my students had a positive reaction to watching words scroll across the screen, seeing little cavemen animate, and observing slides transition in unique ways. Mistakenly, I took this "engagement" in the PowerPoint animations to mean that my students' comprehension of the content was increasing. Thus, I decided to turn all my lectures into PowerPoint presentations. Yet, about three weeks into the PowerPoint lectures, students' heads started dropping back down to their desks, and they no longer cared which animation I chose for a slide or how the words floated across the screen. Their final unit assessment did not show any difference in comprehension of the content from when I did just a traditional lecture. It was my first lesson in how technology can "engage" students in the technology tool, but not necessarily the learning.

When using technology leads to flawed engagement, students will eventually lose interest because they recognize that the technology is a mere trick and not actually adding value to their understanding of the content. After years of watching teachers do the same thing that I had done, I recognized one mechanism lacking in teaching with technology: a practical and measurable framework on what authentic engagement and effective integration look like. For years I was haphazard, trying new technologies because they were shiny and novel, while ignoring or dismissing older ones because we assume "older" equates to antiquated learning. I tried some frameworks (discussed in Chapter 1), but they tended to focus on transforming a task based on a particular tool. Hence, the emphasis was on how extensively one could use the tool, rather than if the tool was helping the students meet their learning outcomes—thus putting the tool before the learning.

I needed a framework that could give me guidance in selecting technology based on the needs of my learners and my instructional goals. Besides knowing how to select the "just right" digital resources, I also needed to know how to use technology tools with students. When my students would use one-to-one devices, I often threw away the effective instructional strategies I knew worked well in a traditional setting. For example, I knew learning was social and knowledge construction happened through social interactions, yet I often isolated students when they were using digital tools and allowed them to sit in corners with headphones on, very rarely having them reflect on their learning experiences within the software. Instead of tossing out those research-based instructional strategies simply because students had a digital device in front of them, I needed to be integrating those strategies into teaching with the technology tools. I had to allow the content learning goals to come before the technology choices, thus enabling the technology tools to support the learning.

Authentic and Measurable Learning with the Triple E Framework

Over the past decade of the digital technology boom in schools, teachers and administrators have witnessed technology being used in superficial ways often enough to know that access to technology in and of itself is not a magic potion. Furthermore, empirical research has also shown that just putting technology into the hands of students does not guarantee improved comprehension of content or learning goals (Conoley, Moore, Croom, & Flowers, 2006; Schackow et al., 2004; Stein, Challman, & Brueckner, 2006, as cited in Filer, 2010). I don't think educators would argue that technology is a tool that should help students reach their learning goals. In life, we don't select a tool and then create a problem just so that we can use the tool; rather we select a tool to meet the needs of the problem. For example, when hanging pictures in my living room, I am not going to use a chainsaw, despite the fanciness of the tool. Instead, I am going to use a basic hammer because it meets my goals. Teaching with technology is also about the operator, not just the tool. Making sure that we put the learning needs of the student before the excitement of the tool is key to successful and effective lessons with technology.

As of 2014, there were over 75,000 apps listed in the education category of the Apple App Store (Wartella, 2015). Yet over 70% of these apps have zero educational research to support their development (Vaala et al., 2015). Very few empirical studies on the use of educational software have been done to show whether the use of such apps correlates with effective learning outcomes (Wartella, 2015). Thus, how does a teacher know which technologies are going to be effective for meeting their students' learning needs? Simply because an education app is featured in the App Store does not mean the app will automatically help students learn. How do we know when we are putting the learning goals first or if the "fun" of swiping and shaking an iPad is actually giving teachers a false sense of "engagement" in the learning goals? How do we measure technology integration in the classroom that goes beyond engagement via access alone?

Educators like myself are often looking for a framework to help answer these questions. There are some helpful frameworks for integrating technology in schools (e.g., TPACK, SAMR, TIM), however many of them lack an explicit practical focus on the learning goals. The primary focus of many frameworks tends to be on comparing the creative use of technology to traditional methods, rather than on how well the tools are able to help students meet the actual learning goals. I would sometimes get lost in these frameworks trying to develop a lesson that creatively uses technology tools in order to meet a higher level of transformation on the models. However, by putting the tool first, the lesson did not always connect to the desired learning outcome, which sometimes became problematic. For example, about two years ago, I learned about a new online gaming tool and decided to try it. I had students participate in the online quiz game to review their understanding of digital safety. The quiz activity was set up in a creative way to get towards a more transformative approach to learning (it even included Skype experts and the option to text a friend). However, I found the students became so fixated on being at the top of the leaderboard in the game that they rushed through the review, did very poor research trying to find correct answers, and would not take the time to reflect on their learning. While the students were focused on the activity, cheering and having a blast, and while I worked hard to set up the game to redefine how they were learning, I realized they were too focused on the tool. I then switched the game back to our old analog system of reflective turn and talks without technology, and I found that they were much more involved in deeper reflection and better meeting the learning goals. It was a reminder to me that trying to reach the upper echelon of a framework by letting the tool lead does not always result in better learning outcomes. The Triple E Framework can help prevent teachers from making some of my mistakes. By using the Triple E Framework alone or in addition to current models, teachers can first, focus on the learning, and second, locate the tools that will help meet the desired learning goals.

The Triple E Framework provides educators with a practical way to measure whether or not authentic student learning is occurring when digital technology tools are integrated into a lesson. It also provides support to help educators make better instructional decisions when integrating digital technology tools. The framework is based on three components: *Engagement* in learning goals, *Enhancement* of learning goals, and *Extension* of learning goals. While these three terms are often used interchangeably, they are distinct and different. This book will define and show examples of what makes each level unique.

What's in This Book

I recommend that readers take a linear approach to this book and read the chapters in order. In doing so, readers will get a full picture of the purpose of the Triple E Framework and what authentic engagement means in educational technology. This book is written as an evolution from theoretical to practical. The chapters evolve, beginning with why the Triple E Framework was created, followed by the research that guides the framework, how it compares to other frameworks, how to use the framework, practical examples of lessons using the framework, and ultimately a lesson-planning template to assist in developing lessons based on the framework. Some educators familiar with the framework may prefer to skip ahead to the examples from the field. In Chapter 8, diverse teachers share their lessons that meet all three elements of the Triple E Framework.

Here is what the reader will find in each chapter:

Chapter 1 includes a brief overview of the current empirical studies on what we know about teaching with technology tools. It is an attempt to shed some light on effective strategies in teaching and learning we can draw from when using technology tools. In addition, the chapter discusses which strategies we should avoid.

Chapter 2 is an overview of popular current frameworks for technology in learning. While there are about a half dozen frameworks, I decided to focus on TPACK, TIM, and SAMR because they are the most well known and are representative of the type of framework we tend to come across. I describe each framework and share how the Triple E Framework can extend the work of these earlier frameworks.

Chapter 3 introduces the Triple E Framework. The framework has been developed based on the research shared in Chapter 1 and throughout the book. Unlike other approaches to technology in learning, this one is based on empirical studies, rather than anecdotes or what "looks good" in the classroom.

Chapters 4, 5, and 6 take a deep dive into defining what the three components of the framework (engagement, enhancement, and extension) should look like in learning with technology tools. Each chapter provides examples of technology tools that integrate the characteristics of their level. Further, the chapters include scenarios of K–12 teaching that measure the technology use in the scenario with the Triple E Framework.

Chapter 7 features the Triple E Framework measurement tool. The tool is open source and easy to use. While not a perfect tool, it gives a benchmark, or guideline, of what educators should consider when developing a lesson with technology tools. This chapter shows teachers how to read the results of the Triple E Framework measurement tool. This chapter also summarizes the scenarios from Chapters 4, 5, and 6 to offer a final analysis of the scenarios based on the measurement tool.

Chapter 8 features case studies of teachers who developed projects that meet all three levels of the Triple E Framework. Some of these cases use very simple technologies (such as email or wikis) while others use more elaborate tools, such as virtual reality. However, the tool does not take center stage in these projects, rather the learning goals and process of learning is key; the technology simply adds value and creates a more authentic experience for the students.

Chapter 9 discusses how to integrate effective instructional strategies when using technology tools for learning. I highlight the notion that for teachers to use effective technology for positive learning goals, effective instructional strategies should be used alongside them. Technology tools cannot do the work of good teaching.

Chapter 10 addresses questions concerning which technology tools are better choices for learning. This chapter takes a look at how teachers can use the Triple E Framework to evaluate individual technology tools for classroom learning. The chapter also shares databases of peer-reviewed tools for education.

Appendix A is a lesson plan template for teachers, administrators, or schools of education to use when planning with technology tools. The lesson plan integrates elements of the Triple E Framework and effective teaching strategies to leverage technology tools in the classroom, allowing teachers to plan for technology use based on good instructional strategies.

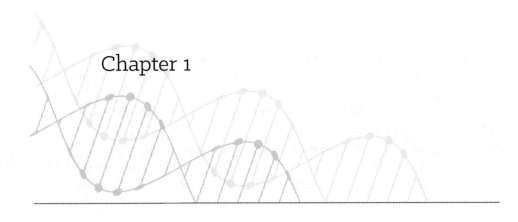

Chapter 1

What We Know About Technology Integration

PRIOR TO USING A FRAMEWORK to measure how well technology supports learning goals, it is important to understand the empirical research on what we already know about technology and student learning. Historically, educational researchers have struggled to find concrete data directly linking a particular technology tool to positive student achievement. Yet, studies over the past two decades have uncovered some pieces of the puzzle to consider when planning for, measuring, and evaluating technology use with students.

This chapter highlights six important themes, based on the research, to consider when integrating technology into learning: Instructional Strategies, Engagement, Access, Application of Use, Authenticity, and Co-Use. This research is the foundation for the Triple E Framework, and it supports the idea that teachers can engage, enhance, and extend learning goals by using instructional moves around technology tools to help students meet those learning goals. Technology alone cannot fully support all learners' needs. (In Chapter 9, I will suggest instructional strategies for integrating technology based on effective methods from the four major content areas.)

Instructional Strategies in Technology Integration

Researchers Mabel Okojie, Anthony Olinzock, and Tinukwa Okojie-Boulder (2006) argue that "the degree of success teachers have in using technology for instruction could depend in part on their ability to explore the relationship between pedagogy and technology." Okojie et al. (2006) contend that perceptions around technology in instruction tend to be narrow and forget to include pedagogical approaches that the teacher implements alongside the technology tools. Technology integration is more complex than simply using a technology tool; pedagogical and instructional strategies around the tool are essential for successful learning outcomes. Okojie et al. (2006) illustrate this point by citing work by Diaz and Bontenbal (2000):

> Using technology to enhance the educational process involves more than just learning how to use [a] specific piece of hardware and software. It requires an understanding of pedagogical principles that are specific to the use of technology in an instructional setting … Pedagogy-based training begins by helping teachers understand the role of learning theory in the design and function of class activities and in the selection and use of instructional technologies. (pp. 2 and 6)

In 2005, Punya Mishra and Matthew Koehler argued there is no one best way to teach with technology; rather, effective technology integration is dependent on the content-specific learning goals and pedagogical strategies used in conjunction with technology to meet those learning goals. It is essential that we look beyond just what the tool itself can do and consider how we can engage with the tool through effective instructional practices to better meet learning goals. Okojie et al. (2006) suggest that teachers consider the following instructional moves when planning for technology tools in the classroom:

- Identify learning objectives and students' needs so that technology tools match the objectives and needs;

- Choose the methods around the technology tools that are relevant to the objectives, the technology selected, learning styles, and modes and pace of learning;

- Design a rich and authentic context around the use of the technology that is dynamic and meaningful to the students;

- Design instruction with the technology tools that provides students with opportunities for problem-solving, inquiry, and analysis.

An essential piece of activating student learning is eliciting their prior knowledge. Constructivists such as Jean Piaget (2013) have long proclaimed that new knowledge is constructed from old knowledge, thus, building on a student's prior knowledge is key to promoting successful cognitive growth. The level of a student's prior knowledge has been found to influence how effective an instructional strategy is for content learning (Kalyuga, Chandler, & Sweller, 2005). Prior knowledge plays a key role in not only traditional learning, but also in predicting learning growth with technology tools (Kalyuga, 2005; Kalyuga, Ayres, Chandler, & Sweller, 2003). In a recent study on students' prior knowledge and technology-mediated learning, researchers found that students with less prior content knowledge performed significantly lower on their assessment outcomes than students with more prior content knowledge, despite using the exact same multimedia learning tool (Rias & Zaman, 2013). This study is a reminder to not assume that technology alone will magically catch up students who have less content knowledge or be able to differentiate to meet them where they are. Researchers have suggested that technology resources and choices should be tailored or differentiated to fit the prior knowledge of the learner, rather than a one-size-fits-all approach (Bell & Kozlowski, 2003). Teachers can make certain that students' prior knowledge, or lack thereof, does not impede how and what they learn with technology tools, by connecting prior knowledge to new learning experiences through instructional strategies such as Know, Wants to Know,

Learned (KWL) charts; brainstorming; or Visible Thinking routines. These strategies can be implemented with technology tools, such as doing a KWL chart by using a piece of software. Or they can also happen in conjunction with the technology, such as doing a mind map on paper before using the technology tool, and periodically pausing to make reflective connections between the content presented by way of technology and the students' prior knowledge.

Engagement

As mentioned in the Introduction, numerous studies have found technology can increase student engagement or motivation. However, research has also uncovered that student engagement does not necessarily lead to positive change in student achievement. For example, the Apple Classrooms of Tomorrow longitudinal 10-year study reported that students in the program (which provided them with an abundance of digital tools) were more engaged when the technology was integrated into the learning experiences compared with the national average of students who were in traditional classrooms; however, while the students' engagement increased, they did not show increased performance on assessment outcomes (Baker et al., 1994; Sandholtz, et al., 1997). Research on student engagement may help us understand why student engagement in technology-enhanced lessons is not necessarily correlating with achievement. Studies on engagement show that while students may be physically present and appear to be actively involved in using the technology tools, in reality they might still be cognitively disengaged from the learning goals (Linnenbrink & Pintrich, 2003). As a result, we mistakenly interpret the extrinsic appearance of student excitement about using the technology tool as actual comprehension of the content learning. Because many studies on student engagement measure engagement by a student's body language and/or through observations on use of the technology tool, it is no surprise that hidden underneath the surface is still a disconnect from the learning goals.

For engagement through technology to be effective, the tool should help focus students' attention on the learning goals and the task at hand rather than distract from it (Wartella, 2015). One element of a truly engaged learner is an environment of active learning. *Active learning* occurs when students are dynamically focused on the learning goals and not just busy doing what looks like learning. According to

Ellen Wartella (2015), "active learning occurs when children are 'minds-on'—that is, engaged in thinking, reflecting, and effortful mental activity...swiping, tapping, and physically engaging with an app is not the same as 'minds-on' activity" (p.1). Hence, the technology is focusing students to be active learners on the learning task—time-on-task—and the teacher should also be using instructional moves to make certain that this is occurring. A few examples of instructional strategies effectively used in conjunction with a technology tool would be monitoring, think-alouds, modeling, and other reflective practices drawn from literacy learning (Duke & Pearson, 2002). Specific instructional strategies will be discussed more in Chapter 9.

Access

An assumption among some educators is that increased access to technology tools will automatically increase student engagement (Richardson & Placier, 2001). The idea is that a student having ubiquitous access to a device will motivate him or her to learn more. Furthermore, students will somehow organically know how to navigate a device for higher cognitive learning experiences. This belief has been debunked by numerous studies, such as one conducted by Loretta Donovan, Tim Green, and Kendall Hartley (2010), which found that increased access to technology does not always lead to an increase in student motivation or engagement. Over the past decade, studies have shown that access to technology tools and resources alone is no guarantee that students' comprehension or academic achievement will increase (Becker, 2000; Fuchs & Woessmann, 2004). Researchers have also found numerous examples of teachers using technology for no other reason than that they were required to by the administration, or wanting to use technology because it looked fun, and often any benefits of that type of technology use were strongly overstated (Cuban, 2001; Oppenheimer, 2003). Many of these teachers had very little to no training in how to select and use technology tools within their content-specific instructional methods.

What about one-to-one schools? Is there a benefit to one device per child? There have been some studies that point to one-to-one device programs being beneficial to student learning outcomes (Barron et al., 2006; Mouza, 2008). However, these studies often bring up the fact that the method in which one-to-one devices are implemented in schools is key for potential success in one-to-one models (Barron et al., 2006). Additionally, most of these studies do not include details of "how" the devices were implemented or the pedagogy around the tool (Zucker, 2004). It is vital that one-to-one schools take into account not just access but how the technology is being implemented in each learning experience for the students (Donovan et al., 2010). Thus, once again the pedagogical and instructional choices around the tools become essential for successful learning outcomes. Schools with one-to-one device access will likely have more success focusing on creating content and learning material around technology tools, rather than using apps and websites with a "drill and practice" approach to learning. A one-to-one school does not automatically correlate to better learning outcomes, as the quality of work done with computers is much more important in determining student achievement than the quantity of time spent with devices (Wenglinsky, 2006).

Application of Use

Many educational software programs use a "drill and practice" approach, in which students read prompts and respond to multiple-choice or closed-ended questions to demonstrate their understanding (Vaala, et al., 2015). Yet, this use of computers as a workbook substitute has not been successful in showing positive achievements for student learning outcomes (Wenglinsky, 1998). Often the use of "drill and practice" software occurs in isolation—teachers trust that the tool alone can teach or reinforce learning concepts and they expect students to navigate the tool on their own. Despite the abundance of software with a "drill and practice" approach, research has shown that technology should be supporting higher-order thinking skills and real-world problem-solving (Roschelle, Pea, Hoadley, Gordin & Means, 2000). Digital technology use for creating and exploring, rather than "drill and practice," has been found to positively affect student achievement, while "drill and practice" tools used in isolation have had few (often no) positive effects on student achievement scores (National Association of Educational Progress, NAEP via Wenglinsky, 2006). Technology tools must encourage meaningful learning, where the technology is extending the learning from students' preexisting knowledge and helping them create new knowledge (Wartella, 2015), rather than just reinforcing old knowledge or only giving students isolated knowledge. Harold Wenglinsky (2006) discovered many secondary teachers were working overtime to come up with creative ways to use novel and interesting technology in their schools. Yet, he cautioned that his studies did not show any evidence that this was the most successful way to use technology in schools:

> The findings of this study suggest that rather than planning lessons around the computer, high school teachers should assume that students will use technology-based tools to address some of their learning tasks. Teachers should not think, *Aha! I will assign a research paper and require students to use the internet to obtain information.* Rather, teachers should assign a research paper and take for granted that students will use computers in a variety of ways to complete the assignment. This approach mirrors the technology-rich work environment in which many students will find themselves after graduation. (p. 32)

It's important that teachers look critically for tools that help students elicit higher-cognitive thinking skills such as inquiry, hypothesis, analysis, and reflective thinking practices. This research reinforces the importance of selecting technology tools to meet learning goals, and integrating good instructional practices around the tool.

Authenticity and Prior Knowledge

Learning should be situated in contexts that are considered real, relational, and substantive (Brown, Collins & Dugid, 1998). Learning situated in authentic contexts has the ability to create "deep learning" in students (Ramsden, 1992). Deep learning can lead to long-term retention and real-world critical application of concepts and ideas. Jean Lave and Etienne Wengner (1991) argued that student learning should be authentically situated in the context of real-world experiences of mathematicians, scientists, writers, and other professions. For years the fields of medical science and education have integrated a very effective apprenticeship model whereby students are placed in authentic professional contexts in order to learn in a professional setting (Boud & Soloman, 2001).

Researchers have found that technology can be used for enabling the creation of authentic tasks and contexts, connecting with outside experts, and creating collaboration across geographic distances (Herrington et al., 2010). A recent study showed that authentic learning supported by emerging technologies with specific pedagogical structures created positive gains for students to become more self-directed learners (Harrington & Parker, 2013). Long-term and sustained learning can happen when technology tools are carefully connected to authentic experiences such as real-life problems, real-life tasks, experts, and communities of practice. The instructional choices that teachers make when integrating technology will determine how deeply students are embedded in the learning process and their long-term retention of the content goals in the experience.

Tips for Successfully Integrating Technology into Lessons

An effective lesson or project that integrates technology should do the following:

- Engage students in time-on-task and mindful activities that help them focus on their learning goals.

- Engage students in becoming active and social learners, through co-use.

- Enhance learning by avoiding isolated use of "drill and practice" software and instead focusing on higher cognitive skills of creating, knowledge gathering, and building.

- Enhance learning by providing scaffolds to connect students' prior knowledge with new knowledge.

- Extend learning to connect students' prior knowledge to their school learning.

- Extend learning by providing opportunities for authentic tasks and contexts to be integrated into classroom learning goals.

The Significance of Co-Use

One instructional approach that has been significant for successful outcomes when using technology is co-use, or co-engagement (Darling-Hammond et al., 2014). Co-use is the person-to-person social use of a digital tool: when a child works together with a parent, teacher, or peer on a digital device. An example would be a teacher and a student working together to navigate a piece of math learning software (rather than the student working alone on the software). Another example would be two students collaborating on a research paper in Google Docs. When co-using a device, students are working with others to figure out how to navigate the content learning within the software, which can lead to higher-order questioning, predicting, inquiry, and other cognitive benefits from this social construction of knowledge. A recent report by the Joan Ganz Cooney Center emphasized the importance of social interactions when learning with technology devices (Vaala et al., 2015). Similar to reading a book with a child (co-reading), researchers have promoted the ability to connect with others through digital media or while using media together as key ways children deepen their learning (e.g., Hirsh-Pasek et al., 2015; Guernsey, 2012; Takeuchi & Stevens, 2011). Northwestern researcher Ellen Wartella (2015) explains that "joint media engagement, and socially interactive learning more generally, offer young children an environment that can help them learn through the Vygotskian notion of scaffolding, or extending children's learning beyond what they would learn left on their own" (p. 1). Digital apps and software are not usually "social" in nature, rather they tend to be created for individual use. Thus, teachers should be thinking about how to develop instructional strategies for co-use with the devices. Some examples include:

- Pairing students so they work together on a learning activity through the device.

- A teacher (or volunteer parents) sitting down periodically with students, asking them questions to check for understanding and making sure they see the connections between the digital tool and their classroom learning goals.

- Sending home short video tutorials for parents to watch so they can learn how to co-use the applications with their children. These videos can include strategies for probing, prompting, and supporting the children in gaining deeper understanding while using the software together.

- Taking the time to give whole-group instruction on not just how to use the tool or software but also how to "think" when using the tool, thus modeling the cognition that you want the students to learn or take up through the digital device.

- Asking students to pair and share what they are learning and how they are learning with the technology tool.

- Inviting children from older grades to come into the classroom to co-use the technology tools with your students. Provide the older children with some prompts and probing questions that they can ask your students while working with them.

- Conducting whole-group interactive share-alouds where students reflect and share what they are learning to the entire class.

Chapter Take-Aways

This chapter provided an overview of the research that has been done on technology and student learning, highlighting six important themes to consider when integrating technology into learning. The findings included here support the idea that teachers can engage, enhance, and extend learning goals by using instructional moves around technology tools to help students meet those learning goals.

- Research shows there are important elements to include when planning for technology use with children.

- Teachers should emphasize quality over quantity when it comes to technology use in schools, because giving students ubiquitous access does not equal better learning.

- Clear instructional strategies need to be used in conjunction with technology tools in order to meet learning goals.

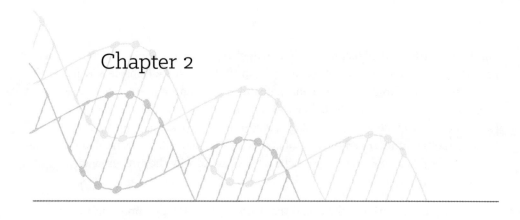

Chapter 2

Building on the Current Frameworks

HISTORICALLY, WHEN new technologies (such as an overhead projector) were introduced to the classroom, these tools tended to continue the stability and transparency of the traditional classroom. Teachers did not have to leave their comfort zone in order to use an overhead projector or slide projector. They were still the sage on the stage and very much in control of the technology. The same cannot be said of most digital technologies being introduced into teaching today. Nowadays, digital tools tend to create disruption and add a new level of complexity to the classroom (Koehler & Mishra, 2009). One of the complexities is assessing how the technology is impacting a student's ability to grasp the learning goals.

For decades, educational technology has struggled to develop a solid theoretical and practical framework for technology integration (Roblyer, 2005; Roblyer & Knezek, 2003). Researchers continue to lament that studies examining preservice teachers' development of technology skills lack a clearly articulated theoretical framework (Mishra & Khoeler, 2006). Mabel Okojie, Anthony Olinzock, and Tinukwa Okojie-Boulder (2006) summarized the lack of clarity in a framework for technology integration in their observation of teachers being asked why they integrate technology in their classrooms:

> A great majority of them said that they use technology (more specifically computers) for instruction because it helps teachers to teach and students to learn. This response is too general and does not convey an in-depth understanding of technology integration. These students fail to articulate in any meaningful way how technology can be used to improve learning. Their response does not capture the intricate relationship between pedagogy and technological resources. Lack of appropriate guidelines limits teachers' use of technology for instruction, and limits their desire to explore the use of technology beyond basic applications. (p. 69)

Despite teachers claiming that technology helps students learn, education lacks a tool to measure if and how learning is occurring as a result of using technology. Educators who do use a framework often point to a variety of frameworks when asked about how they integrate technology. This chapter will discuss some of the more prevalent frameworks that educators use for integrating technology in learning. The chapter will also discuss how the Triple E Framework can be an extension to address the gaps in these current frameworks. The frameworks discussed in this chapter are by no means all of the frameworks in use, but they are representative of the types of frameworks currently used in education technology.

TPACK Framework

The Technological Pedagogical Content Knowlege (TPACK) model was developed around 2005–2006 by Punya Mishra and Matthew Koehler at Michigan State University. This model is a big-picture conceptual view of how technology could be integrated into the classroom. In 2005, Mishra and Koehler argued that there is no one best way to teach with technology, rather it is dependent on each subject matter's learning goals. Thus, they claimed that good teaching is about content, pedagogy, and technology and the relationships between them. Based on this argument, Mishra and Koehler (2005) developed the theoretical framework, which focuses on the integration of technological, pedagogical, and content knowledge (TPCK was redefined as TPACK by Thompson & Mishra in 2007). TPACK asserts that the interaction of technological knowledge (TK), pedagogical knowledge (PK), content knowledge (CK), pedagogical content knowledge (PCK), technological content knowledge (TCK), and technological pedagogical knowledge (TPK) produces technological pedagogical and content knowledge (TPACK). See Figure 2.1 for a visual concept of the TPACK model.

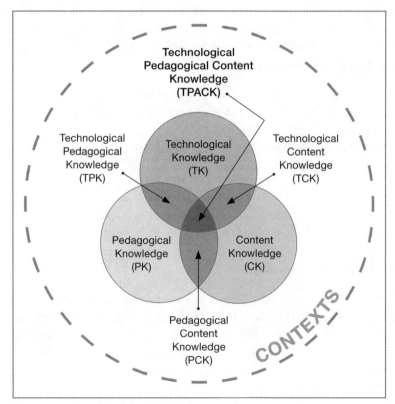

Figure 2.1 A model of the TPACK framework

The TPACK framework models the type of flexible knowledge needed to success-fully integrate technology use into teaching (Mishra & Koehler, 2009). It considers meaningful use of technology in the classroom to require teachers to integrate technological affordances with pedagogical approaches for the specific subject matter to be taught (Mishra & Khoeler, 2006). TPACK asks educators to use their content knowledge, pedagogical knowledge, and technology knowledge to guide their students in meeting specific classroom learning goals. Having a mastery over all three areas will help guide teachers to effectively integrate technology into their lesson plans. For example, a social studies lesson about primary resources may require students to support their hypotheses with evidence they find in documents. Thus, the teacher may want to locate a tool online that will aid students in both locating primary resources and identifying and/or storing the evidence they find in those documents. Thus, TPACK is a useful model for thinking about the "big picture" of what a teacher needs to know in order to better integrate technology. In Chapter 1, we discussed that researchers have been clear about the need to build pedagogical structures around technology tools and not have students using them in isolation; this model really speaks to that need.

While educators were originally quick to adopt TPACK, they are now getting stuck at what TPACK looks like in the K–12 classroom and how to measure success in technology-infused lessons (Angeli & Valanides, 2009; Archambault & Barnett, 2010; Graham, 2011; Jimoyiannis, 2010). Charoula Angeli & Nicos Valanides (2009) directly addressed the challenge in the TPACK framework:

> While it is perfectly understood that the preference for a general
> model might be directly related to its potential wide applicability in
> different contexts, the lack of specificity is problematic, because the
> very important issue of how tool affordances can transform content
> and pedagogy is not addressed. (p. 157)

Researchers have become more critical of TPACK as a workable framework for measuring effective technology integration. There has been an appeal from educators for a practical framework wherein elements of the TPACK framework are present but not overly complicated (Angeli & Valanides, 2009). There is also a need for a frame-work that focuses specifically on measuring the impact technology has on students' ability to take up the content-based learning goals. While TPACK is an excellent conceptual framework, it needs the addition of a practical tool to help teachers make transparent the connections between effective pedagogical moves, content, and technology. The Triple E Framework was created based on this need to extend TPACK to a measurable framework. (For more information, see www.tpack.org.)

TIM Framework

The Technology Integration Matrix (TIM) was developed around 2005 by a team at the University of South Florida College of Education. The model includes five characteristics of meaningful learning environments: active, constructive, goal-directed, authentic, and collaborative. TIM takes a practical look at how technology is being used in the classroom. Besides the characteristics of meaningful learning environments, the model also considers five levels of technology integration: entry, adoption, adaptation, infusion, and transformation. The model is built on a matrix approach, in which the goal appears to be reaching the transformation level of technology integration and meeting all five characteristics of a meaningful learning environment. The matrix is meant to be a measurable "guide" for educators integrating technology.

The TIM is a solid model and can be useful for educators who are focused on "how" the technology interacts with the students. However, the main focus of TIM is not on the learning goals, but rather on how the technology is used with students and if the tools are integrated in a sophisticated way. While not insignificant, notice that there are five levels and five types of measurements, which often have very nuanced differences (some almost no difference), effectively making this model more cumbersome and time-consuming when evaluating the technology use. With all that said, the matrix can be a useful way to consider technology adoption levels and how they relate to types of use in the classroom, but it is difficult to measure how effective the technology is at meeting the content-specific learning goals and outcomes. Therefore, the Triple E Framework helps extend this model by integrating some of the meaningful learning strategies from the model into a framework that also looks at how these strategies are used to meet targeted learning goals. (For more information, see fcit.usf.edu/matrix/matrix.)

SAMR Model

The Substitution, Augmentation, Modification, and Redefinition (SAMR) model (Figure 2.2) was developed by Dr. Ruben Puentedura in 2012. Similar to TPACK, this model has been quickly embraced by teachers. Unlike some frameworks with a complex measurement matrix, SAMR is a simple model to follow. A teacher can easily plug specific technology tools into the model's various levels. The SAMR model is attractive in that it considers how the technology tool is being used in the classroom setting and is based on four types of technology use: substitution, augmentation, modification, and redefinition.

At the first level, substitution, the teacher considers whether the technology is being used to "substitute" a traditional tool, such as a student using an interactive whiteboard to write down lecture notes instead of a traditional chalkboard. The replacement of the chalkboard with an interactive whiteboard does not change the activity that the teacher or student is doing; the activity is simply done on a different device. At the second level, augmentation, the teacher considers if the technology is used to "augment" a traditional activity. An example of augmentation would be having students draw a picture using an iPad, which gives them more options for drawing, such as adding clip art to the story when they doodle. This is an activity that would be more difficult to do with just a piece of paper. Thus the activity is being augmented or slightly boosted because of the technology. The third level considers whether the technology tool is being used to "modify" a traditional classroom tool or task. An example of modification would be redesigning the task of a traditional cooperative group jigsaw, so instead of having students write their own notes and share back with smaller groups, they would use Google Docs to collaborate on one large set of notes together. The addition of Google Docs helps to augment the type of activity students are doing with the tools. Finally, at the last level the teacher considers whether the technology "redefines" a task; that is, whether the actual task completely changes as a result of the technology tool. For example, instead of writing a letter to an author's publisher and hoping for a response, a classroom could tweet the author (such as @judybloom) and ask to set up a Skype conversation with her!

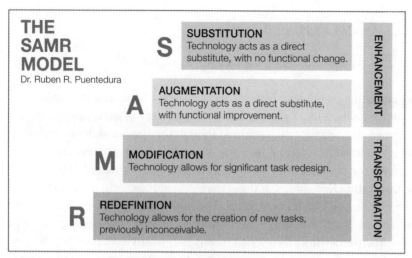

Figure 2.2 A model of the SAMR framework

The SAMR model is helpful in explaining how the technology is utilized differently than traditional teaching tools and how it sometimes can change the nature of the lesson itself. Yet, there has been confusion concerning whether the model is meant to be a hierarchy of levels, or a straight line with no hierarchy and just categories. Either way, one major element that could be added to this model is how the technology addresses the learning goals; some experts have noted that even if the lesson achieves redefinition with the tools, the correlation to meeting the actual learning goals is not always present (November, 2015). SAMR does not directly address how the learning goals play a role in the technology choice. While a teacher could be using technology to "redefine" a task, such as having students make QR codes for all of their reflections on their mathematical learning, one needs to ask if the QR codes improve or enhance the students' understanding of the Common Core State Standards for Mathematics. I am not sure it is any better than having students write down their reflections or discuss them in class. We want to make certain that when we look at the SAMR model, we also are considering the learning outcomes and not just the unique ways that the technology tools are changing the way classroom activities happen. The Triple E Framework helps extend the SAMR model by making these connections.

A Framework That Focuses on Learning Goals

One aspect of education technology integration that most educators agree upon is that technology should be a tool to help students reach learning goals (Becker, 2000). Studies have shown that teachers do not feel as though they have a skill set or clear framework to understand how to best measure whether technology tools are helping students meet learning outcomes (Firek, 2003; Ertmer, 1999; Swanson, 2006). Additionally, integrating technology in the classroom requires a unique understanding of how technology tools can constrain or enable one's effort to meet specific learning goals (Neiss, 2005). Teaching with technology is about the learning first and the tool second. The frameworks mentioned in this chapter all have clear benefits, particularly in planning for technology use or in considering "how" the technology is modifying traditional classroom activities and routines. In order to extend these frameworks, the Triple E model was developed to work with or without the current frameworks in order to do the following:

- Integrate the current research on characteristics of effective teaching and learning strategies with technology tools.

- Focus specifically on how the technology is meeting the needs of the learner.

- Be user-friendly for a quick evaluation.

- Be able to evaluate both lesson plans and technology tools, looking for effective learning strategies built into both.

- Consider and leave room for pedagogical strategies to work with technology tools, rather than looking at technology tools in isolation.

The next chapter will outline the Triple E Framework, which was developed at the University of Michigan based on the current research around technology use in learning.

Chapter Take-Aways

This chapter provided an overview of the existing frameworks for technology integration and offered insights into how the Triple E Framework can improve and extend learning by focusing on learning goals and evaluating student outcomes.

- TPACK is a useful theoretical framework for how to think about technology integration, but struggles as a practical "how to" guide.

- SAMR and TIM are both helpful practical frameworks, yet they tend to focus on the tool first (as well as other pieces, such as the teacher's comfort with technology) and learning goals second.

- The Triple E takes the strongest pieces of these frameworks and weaves them into a practical measurement tool that focuses on the learning goals before the technology tool.

Chapter 3

The Triple E Framework and the ISTE Student Standards

ONE OF THE CRITICISMS of technology use in school learning is that it is an "add on," something that teachers only use *IF* there is extra time or *IF* they want to. Historically, technology-integrated learning has not been considered essential. Many educators have found that they are able to meet the content-specific learning goals without the aid of technology.

However, it's important to remember that instead of integrating technology to falsely engage or "drill and practice" students, technology should be helping students meet learning goals in ways that they could not easily do without the tools. Technology in schools should be integrated mindfully with time-on-task active learning, stressing quality over quantity, co-use over individual, creating, problem-solving, and connecting prior real-world knowledge to learning. Technology can and should be adding value to leverage how learning goals are met. The Triple E Framework encourages teachers to look beyond artificial engagement or substitution of traditional tools and consider how technology could push students into a direction that enhances and extends the content-specific learning goals.

Components of the Framework

The Triple E Framework attempts to define what it looks like to effectively integrate technology tools into a lesson while supporting learning goals. The Framework is based on three components: **Engagement** in learning goals, **Enhancement** of learning goals, and **Extension** of learning goals. While these three terms are often used interchangeably, they are distinct, and it is important to define and show examples of what makes each level unique. This chapter outlines each of the three components of the framework, and the following three chapters explain each part of the framework in detail, giving examples of how the framework can be used in K–12 teaching.

Engagement is the first measure of the Framework. This component considers how the technology tools are helping students focus on the learning goals and tasks. As mentioned in the Introduction, teachers should be wary of false engagement and try to avoid it. It is essential that engagement through technology is time-on-task, actively focused on learning goals, and allows students to participate in active social learning (through co-use or co-engagement). Time-on-task is present when the learning activity with the tool focuses the student on the actual process of learning and not just swiping through a device. For example, a student using an app to create a storybook about a famous person may be occupied and focused on the app. However, if their activity time is spent giving their characters silly faces and has nothing to do with their biography goals, then they are not time-on-task with their learning goals through the device. Instructional strategies should be put in place around the tool to make certain that authentic engagement is occurring (these strategies will be discussed in Chapter 9). This active and mindful engagement should lead to increased comprehension. Once students have active and social engagement, we can consider the other two measures of the Framework.

Enhancement is the second component of the Framework. Enhancement considers how technology tools help students develop an understanding of the learning goals that they could not otherwise have achieved. In other words, what is the added value of using technology tools? Enhancement could mean the technology supports co-use, active learning, differentiation, personalization, higher-level thinking skills, and real-world connections in ways that traditional tools could not. For example, a technology tool may provide personalized scaffolds to support students and give them feedback as they move through a piece of software. (Note that these scaffolds may be more difficult for a teacher to provide in a classroom of 30 students.)

Extension is the third component of the Framework. Extension reflects how well technology creates a bridge between classroom learning and everyday lives. For example, a classroom could use authentic data from a live web feed on the county-by-county local election results to help students learn about how local elections work. Extension also considers how students can develop soft skills that will be useful in their everyday lives.

An exemplary lesson plan combines all three Framework components, engaging students in learning goals, enhancing those learning goals, and extending the learning goals into everyday life (Figure 3.1). Not every lesson plan needs to meet all three parts, but considering each of these E's is a helpful guideline when planning with technology tools to meet learning goals.

Point A is a lesson that integrates technology but does not have any of the three components. An example is a lesson in which students are expected to learn and differentiate the sounds of letters by individually playing an iPad game. The game requires them to trace letters but provides no sound effects. The game's lack of sound and phonetic illustrations prevents students from being co-engaged—they do not focus on the learning task and may be easily distracted by the game approach to the software.

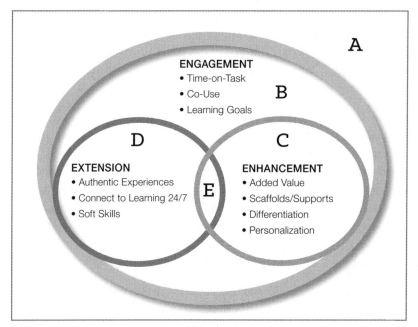

Figure 3.1 This diagram demonstrates how the three Triple E components merge in an ideal lesson or project. Note that it is rare that such a lesson will not have engagement if the other two components are present.

Point B is a lesson that only has engagement, but no enhancement or extension of the learning. An example would be a lesson in which students, working in pairs, use their cell phones to quickly answer "drill and practice" questions on mathematical problems in algebra and send their answers to their teacher (the teacher provides no feedback). They are co-engaged with the tool, and hopefully the co-engagement and the monitoring of their activities by the teacher (who receives their answers) keeps them on task. But there are no connections to how these questions relate to students' authentic lives, and the technology is not directly giving them enhanced opportunities to engage in higher-level thinking.

Point C is a lesson that could be engaging and enhance learning goals but still may not extend learning to making authentic connections to everyday life. For example, students could be working in teams using an app on their iPad to learn about the electoral process. The app helps to scaffold the students' understanding of how their representatives are elected because as they progress through the simulated game, they are asked to reflect on their activities in an electronic notebook. However, the software does not necessarily directly connect to how the electoral process affects their everyday lives. The students are co-using the software with their team members, and the software enhances understanding by providing scaffolds to support learning (such as the reflective notebook), but the app does not directly connect life civics learning to students' local, state, or federal representatives.

Point D is a lesson that could be engaging and extend learning into the authentic world but not really scaffold the understanding. For example, if students were asked to do a video-based discussion with Bill Nye for science, the lesson might create an authentic learning experience by having a real science expert virtually join them, but it might not create any unique scaffolds to help students better understand the content.

Point E represents a high level of thoughtful technology integration, wherein the technology is engaging, enhancing, and extending the learning goals. For example, a journalism teacher who wants their students to work in reporting teams to understand live reporting may create a blog where students can send in live video, audio, or text reports from their cell phones as they are interviewing people in the local community. The students may also download an app on their phone that allows them to do synchronous and easy video, audio, and text editing with other students in their reporting team. Thus, they can be co-editing their report from their phones wherever they are! The students are co-engaging by using their devices to interview others, and they are using it in a way that is focused in real time on the learning goals. The students' learning is enhanced because it would be very difficult to engage in this form of creation, questioning, and reflection without the mobile phones to help collect the data. The students' learning goals are extended because they are using the technology tool to interview authentic people in their everyday lives, thus learning how to use technology tools to leverage communication and publication skills.

Triple E Framework Terms

Engage

- The technology allows students to *focus* on the assignment or activity with less distraction (time-on-task).

- The technology *motivates* students to start the learning process.

- The technology causes a *shift in the behavior* of the students, where they go from being passive to active social learners (co-use/co-engagement).

Enhance

- The technology allows students to *develop a more sophisticated understanding* of the learning goals or content (higher-level thinking skills).

- The technology creates ways *(scaffolds)* to make it easier to understand concepts or ideas.

- The technology creates paths for students to *demonstrate their understanding of the learning goals* in a way that they could not do with traditional tools.

Extend

- The technology creates opportunities for students to *learn outside of their typical school day* (24/7 learning).

- The technology helps *create a bridge* between students' school learning and their everyday life experiences.

- The technology allows students to grow as learners in a lifelong way, so they do not need the school setting to continue to use the tools.

How the Framework Aligns with the ISTE Student Standards

Lesson designs that integrate technology should include connections to the ISTE student standards. The three components of the Triple E Framework—engagement, enhancement, and extension of learning—are directly connected with the 2016 ISTE Standards for Students. Table 3.1 outlines how the ISTE standards connect with the three components of the Triple E Framework.

Table 3.1 Connecting the Triple E Framework to the ISTE Standards for Students

Standard	Engagement	Enhancement	Extension
Empowered Learner	Students use technology to work together (with time-on-task) on building communities of practice, trouble-shooting technology, and seeking feedback to improve their understanding.	Students' learning experiences are personalized and customized for and by the learner with the aid of technology tools.	Students are able to connect their understanding of the learning goals with happenings in their everyday lives through various technologies.
Digital Citizen	Students are able to use technology to not only construct their digital identities but also help others maintain safe, legal, positive, and ethical identities through co-engagement by setting up profiles and monitoring digital posts.	Students are able to add value to their digital identities by utilizing technology tools that allow them to secure personal privacy and security settings, as well as engaging in positive, safe, ethical, and legal behavior online.	Students are able to maintain and contribute to keeping their digital identities positive. They also understand the connection their online footprint has to their everyday life.

Continued

Standard	Engagement	Enhancement	Extension
Knowledge Constructor	Students are active, hands-on with technology tools that evaluate and analyze the accuracy of information. They are building knowledge with others through technology tools, rather than just consuming knowledge.	Students are able to construct and co-construct knowledge, and search for and evaluate information through technology more easily than they could without the technology tools.	Students are able to utilize technology tools to construct knowledge around real-world problems that helps them make sense of their world.
Innovative Designer	Students co-use digital tools to generate ideas and open-ended questions, and create artifacts in the design process.	Students use digital tools to add value by scaffolding the research and organization of the design process.	Students use technology to help identify and solve authentic problems through a deliberate design process.
Computational Thinker	Students use technology tools to co-engage with others in analyzing and representing data.	Students use digital technologies to scaffold the process of understanding data by breaking it down and analyzing it.	Students use technology to collect and investigate authentic data, to look for real-world solutions, and to represent findings in authentic ways.
Creative Communicator	Students use digital technologies to co-create original works and actively share their learning through a choice of tools.	Students utilize digital technologies that enable them to purposefully and carefully communicate complex ideas through original works and visualizations.	Students use digital technologies to make sense of complex ideas by connecting to the world around them.
Global Collaborator	Students use technology to co-engage and co-construct knowledge with other learners outside of their classroom to collaborate on learning goals.	Students utilize technology to add value (in a way they could not do without technology) to their understanding of local and global issues.	Students use technology to explore authentic local and global issues, connecting learning goals to everyday life.

Chapter Take-Aways

This chapter provides an overview of the Triple E Framework, which encourages teachers to consider how technology can push students in a direction that enhances and extends content-specific learning goals.

- Technology tools should be integrated only after learning goals are defined.

- Technology tools should engage students in learning through time-on-task activities that allow the students to become active and social learners.

- Technology tools should add value, such as supports (scaffolds), to enhance students' learning experience in ways that could not easily be done without those tools.

- Technology tools should extend student learning in order to connect classroom content learning to authentic tasks and contexts.

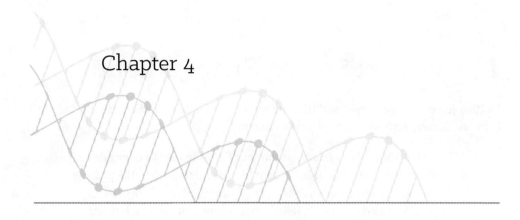

Chapter 4

Defining Engagement

CHAPTERS 2 AND 3 shared how engagement has stood out for decades in education as an essential element for successful student learning with technology tools. This chapter will highlight other research in education that supports the need for integrating technology to create the authentic engagement that allows students to become active, social, and focused learners.

Active and Social Engagement

In 1966 Jerome Bruner explained that the essence of teaching and learning is to help learners become actively involved in the content:

> To instruct someone … is not a matter of getting him to commit results to mind. Rather, it is to teach him to participate in the process that makes possible the establishment of knowledge. We teach a subject not to produce little living libraries on that subject, but rather to get a student to think mathematically for himself, to consider matters as an historian does, to take part in the process of knowledge-getting. Knowing is a process not a product. (p. 72)

Based on Bruner's above description of engagement, part of measuring engagement must consider whether or not students are dynamically involved in the learning processes. A key element of engagement is that students are "active" in the learning process (Prince, 2004; Pike, Kuh, & McCormick, 2008). Student engagement includes students being hands-on in knowledge gathering and dissemination. Thus, engagement is not just about holding students' attention, it is also about shifting them from being passive to active learners in the classroom content and learning goals. Linda Darling-Hammond et al. (2008) explains that active learning practices have a larger impact on student performance than any other variable in the learning, including student background. In addition, as mentioned in Chapter 1, there should be a social aspect to the learning process (such as co-use), whereby the student is working with others (e.g., a peer, a parent, or a teacher) to actively learn with the technology tool. For years, educational researchers have found that the social part of learning was crucial to fully engage students in learning goals (Vygotsky, 1978; Bruner, 1966). When technology tools have been thoughtfully deployed with active and social use in the classroom, student engagement is associated with positive learning outcomes (Chen, Lambert, & Guidry, 2010; Nelson Laird & Kuh, 2005; Prince, 2004).

Time-on-Task: Focus on Learning Goals

In addition to being hands-on, engagement means students are motivated to immerse themselves in the content learning. Thoughtfully deployed technology should meet the needs of the learners and not distract them from the learning goals (Linnenbrink & Pintrich, 2003). Teachers should develop strategies to help students stay focused as the instruction progresses (Okojie et al., 2006). For example, a teacher can use guided practice to model how students should navigate a piece of software that will help them revise their writing, and give them specific ways to think about the activities within the software, such as, "When you see the pictures, do a search for one of your keywords, and select the image that best represents the meaning in your text. Avoid selecting a picture just because you like it." As previously mentioned, the technology alone will not automatically create truly engaged learners; teachers need to integrate good instructional strategies to help create authentic engagement.

What does it mean to engage students in learning? The Triple E Framework defines engagement as students becoming active, social, and focused learners of the content goals. Engaging students with technology means integrating technology that allows students to *focus* on the assignment task or activity with less distraction, that *motivates* them to start the learning process, and that causes a *shift in students' behavior* in which they go from being passive to active social learners.

Strategies to Promote Engagement

Some technology tools are not created for co-use or as supports for time-on-task. Hence, teachers need to integrate good instructional practices to promote student engagement. Early literacy experts Nell Duke and David Pearson (2002) advocate for sound instructional practices that help students learn how to read. Those same instructional practices can be used for engaging students in learning through the technology tools.

Here are a few examples:

- Guided practice

- "I do, we do, you do"

- Co-reading or co-engagement

- Monitoring

Table 4.1 Engagement Take-Away Strategies

Characteristic of Engagement	When Instructional Strategies for Engagement Are Built into Tool	When Instructional Strategies for Engagement Are NOT Built into Tool
Social, Co-Use, or Co-Engagement	Students co-construct knowledge or collaborate with other students in the tool. Students collaborate with experts or parents who are communicating via the tool. Teachers work through the tool to monitor and engage with students as they work.	Pair students up using the tool. Teachers model how to navigate and think with the tool: "I do, we do, you do." Teachers or parents use guided practice to work with students on how to navigate and think as they use the tool.
Active Learning	The technology forces students to be hands-on in investigating and constructing their understanding of the learning goals. The technology allows students to self-pace through the tool, with supports to stay on the learning task.	Use think-aloud or share-aloud sessions (students periodically pause and reflect and share what they are learning with others). Use reflective thinking practices.
Time-on-Task	The tool provides supports to stay on the learning task. Reflective practices are built into learning in the tool.	Students complete paper handouts and checklists as they navigate a tool. Conduct teacher think-alouds. Use a software tour.

Note: Strategies for "outside of the tool" are explained in detail in Chapter 9.

Table 4.1 shows what the characteristics of engagement may look like when the technology tool has organically built-in features of engagement. For example, a piece of software may allow students to collaborate on a shared document, thus allowing them to work independently on their own tool but still use the software to collaborate with their classmates on their work. The table also shows instructional strategies for creating engagement around the use of the technology tool when engagement is not present within the tool. For example, students working on a "drill and practice" piece of software could be paired up to do the activities together and then periodically stop and share aloud what they are learning. (In Chapter 9, more examples of effective instructional practices with technology tools will be fleshed out.)

A Look at Tools That Promote Engagement

Teachers can use effective instructional strategies to promote engagement, such as pairing students up while using a piece of software or using a guided practice approach and modeling for students what to think about when using the technology tool. However, some technology tools are created with these practices in mind and have built-in engagement features of time-on-task and co-use (Chapter 10 details how to evaluate software applications based on the Triple E Framework). Table 4.2 shows a few examples of software that have organically built-in engagement features.

Table 4.2 Technology Tools with Built-in Characteristics of Engagement

Name of Tool	Co-Use	Time-on-Task	Content Area	Cost
Google Docs/ Slides/Sheets	Google tools are built for collaboration. They allow multiple editors to edit the same resource and have a history so that all the contributions from each editor are visible.	There is more focus placed on the process of learning (with the editing and commenting tools), rather than a beautiful product in the end.	ALL	Free

Continued

Name of Tool	Co-Use	Time-on-Task	Content Area	Cost
Write About	Write About is built on the idea that learning to write requires collaboration, scaffolds, and revision, thus the tool has features for co-editing. Peers, teachers, and even outside experts weigh in on a student's writing process. Teachers can also give real-time feedback as students are writing.	The software has built-in supports that help the students focus on the task of learning to write, including story ideas and a process for getting synchronous feedback from instructors. There are few distractions.	ELA	Free
Popplet	Popplet is a graphic organizing tool with built-in tools for collaborative brainstorming. Students co-construct knowledge and document who is sharing what and when.	There is a time-warp feature that aids in documenting and archiving students' progress, which can also help them focus on the task at hand.	ALL	Free
Soundtrap	Soundtrap is a cloud-based collaborative music-editing tool. Students can work with other music editors at the same time to build out a song or podcast.	The only option in the software is to build music and audio feeds. There are no distractions (e.g., rewards or games).	ALL/ Music/ Arts	Free
Spacedeck	Spacedeck is a collaborative whiteboard. It allows multiple editors to work together. Teachers can upload images, PDFs, videos and other supports to help scaffold understanding and instruction.	The whiteboard does have many types of tools for students to co-construct their learning.	ALL	Free

Continued

Name of Tool	Co-Use	Time-on-Task	Content Area	Cost
Pear Deck	Pear Deck is a website and app that is used as an interactive lecture tool. Students follow along and participate in activities in the tool in real time (or self-paced). Teachers can see and interact with students as they are showing and sharing their understanding.	Teachers can get real-time feedback from students as well as share feedback with students during lectures. With Pear Deck, students go from being passive to active learners in the lecture process.	ALL	Free and Premium levels
Drawtime and Storytime by Kindoma	Kindoma is an early literacy software company that uses research on co-engagement strategies to help young children co-read and co-construct knowledge with adults using drawing tools and video.	Children co-engage with parents, mentors, teachers, or older siblings through the tool as they talk about their learning.	Early Literacy	Free

Scenarios of Engagement

Here are three questions, developed as part of the Triple E Framework, to ask when measuring for engagement in learning goals through a technology tool.

1. Does the technology allow students to focus on the assignment or activity with less distraction?

2. Does the technology motivate students to start the learning process of knowledge gathering?

3. Does the technology cause a shift in the behavior of the students, where they go from being passive to active social learners?

Using the three questions, consider if engagement is present in the following teaching and learning scenarios.

Scenario 1

A second-grade teacher presenting a unit on ecosystems gives student pairs iPads that are preloaded with software for exploring various ecosystems in 3D. The software uses authentic images and live webcams from real ecosystems around the world, allowing students to click and tap on animals and plants in the ecosystems to learn more about them. The software also has a recorded notebook feature that lets students audio record oral observations, paste in images from the software, or type their scientific observations.

Learning Goal: Students will develop a hypothesis around what types of plants and animals live in different ecosystems and record their hypothesis with evidence to corroborate their thoughts.

1. **Does the technology allow students to focus on the assignment or activity with less distraction?**

    Yes. The software only has a focus on the ecosystems and students are locked into the app.

2. **Does the technology motivate students to start the learning process of knowledge gathering?**

    Yes. The software is aesthetically pleasing to the eye, and by using the recorded notebook they can begin to gather their evidence immediately.

3. **Does the technology cause a shift in the behavior of the students, where they go from being passive to active social learners?**

    Yes. The software asks students to be hands-on by exploring various ecosystems while tapping, swiping, and recording observations. The teacher also sets it up for co-use by pairing students to work together.

Scenario 2

A teacher asks students to use math software on individual desktop computers. The software allows the teacher to program differentiated learning paths for each student so that when they log in, they are working in their individual zones of proximal development (ZPD). The software uses simulations and videos with short-answer explanations rather than "drill and practice" questions, and it allows the teacher to provide immediate feedback (synchronously) as students take different assessments in a game-like format.

Learning Goal: Students will be able to show their understanding of how to calculate the surface area and perimeter of geometry shapes by participating in mathematical assessment of geometric figures.

1. **Does the technology allow students to focus on the assignment or activity with less distraction?**

   Yes. The software only has a focus on the math and learning goals, and while it is game-based, students must complete responses and have them checked by the teacher before moving on.

2. **Does the technology motivate students to start the learning process of knowledge gathering?**

   Yes. The software is aesthetically pleasing to the eye with a game-like format, but most importantly, the teacher can synchronously check in on work to make sure students are not rushing through the game.

3. **Does the technology cause a shift in the behavior of the students, where they go from being passive to active social learners?**

   Yes. The software asks students to be hands-on by doing math and participating in the mathematical problems, and there is co-use with the teacher, who checks for understanding and gives immediate feedback as students are working.

Scenario 3

A social studies teacher is conducting a lecture by projecting a slideshow on static presentation software. The lecture is on visual inquiry, and the students are listening to and watching the presentation without technology in their hands; only the teacher is using technology.

Learning Goal: Students will understand how to do visual inquiry on images from the Revolutionary War time period. They will be able to understand the skill of visual inquiry and apply inquiry to any image.

1. **Does the technology allow students to focus on the assignment or activity with less distraction?**

   Somewhat. The teacher will control the images and slides shown, which may cut down on students using their own technology to distract themselves. However, students could still disengage from the lecture.

2. **Does the technology motivate students to start the learning process of knowledge gathering?**

   No. The students have no control or say in the technology and the way it is used, thus is it not likely to be any more motivating to start learning than a straight lecture with textbook images.

3. **Does the technology cause a shift in the behavior of the students, where they go from being passive to active social learners?**

   No. The students are simply watching a slideshow and listening to a lecture; they are not hands-on with the technology or working with others through the technology.

Scenario 4

A kindergarten teacher focusing on early literacy goals of writing capital letters has each student come up to the interactive whiteboard to trace letters with the whiteboard pens.

Learning Goal: Students will be able to recognize letters and properly write capital letters.

1. **Does the technology allow students to focus on the assignment or activity with less distraction?**

   Yes. The software provides a template with specific tracings on the board and the teacher is overseeing the work.

2. **Does the technology motivate students to start the learning process of knowledge gathering?**

   Yes. The software allows each student to take a turn tracing the letter, although not all students can participate at the same time.

3. **Does the technology cause a shift in the behavior of the students, where they go from being passive to active social learners?**

Somewhat. The software asks students to be hands-on as they do the tracing. It may lead to a social feature, where the teacher discusses with students what they are doing. However, not all the students can do the tracings at the same time, and it depends on how the teacher structures the discussion around the letters. The interactive whiteboard is not social in nature.

Scenario 5

A social studies and mathematics teacher has students working in pairs to use a website that is tracking the live primary election results. The students are posting their predictions into a Google Sheets collaborative spreadsheet to share what they think will happen in the next hours of voting based on the real-time voting results. The students then set up the spreadsheet equation editor to calculate how far off their predictions were as the live results come in.

Learning Goal: Students will be able to understand how to make predictions in mathematics.

1. **Does the technology allow students to focus on the assignment or activity with less distraction?**

    Yes. The website has live results that are being used to make and elicit student predictions. The Google Sheets spreadsheet keeps students focused on the process of building out their predictions and not on a shiny or fancy tool.

2. **Does the technology motivate students to start the learning process of knowledge gathering?**

    Yes. The website and Google Sheets allow students to begin the process of mathematical predicting.

3. **Does the technology cause a shift in the behavior of the students, where they go from being passive to active social learners?**

    Yes. The students are not just watching the election results, they are actually putting them into a spreadsheet to make quick predications and co-using the software by talking and debating with their partner about their predictions. They are also collaborating through the software by viewing and commenting on each other's predictions.

Scenario 6

An English teacher asks students to use a static ebook app on their iPads that explains how to write a five-paragraph essay. Each student has his or her own iPad and swipes through after reading each page. When students finish, they get their name on top of a leaderboard if they finish reading in under 15 minutes. Then the students start working on their five-paragraph essay (using pen and paper).

Learning Goal: Students will learn how to write a five-paragraph essay.

1. **Does the technology allow students to focus on the assignment or activity with less distraction?**

   Somewhat. Students could be reading the text, but they could easily just be swiping through the software to get a quicker time on the leaderboard without really learning how to write the five-paragraph essay.

2. **Does the technology motivate students to start the learning process of knowledge gathering?**

   Somewhat. While students are possibly reading the text, they are not doing anything to show their understanding while reading.

3. **Does the technology cause a shift in the behavior of the students, where they go from being passive to active social learners?**

   No. The students are not using the tool to interact with content, just to read. There is no social or co-use aspect to this activity.

Scenario 7

A fifth-grade teacher focusing on multiplying fractions asks students to each use interactive screencasting software on an iPad to show how they solve a problem. Students can record their own screens as they solve the math problem, and they can use the text and drawing tools simultaneously to show their mathematical thinking behind each step. The recording is sent to the teacher.

Learning Goal: Students will understand how to multiply fractions and show their work.

1. **Does the technology allow students to focus on the assignment or activity with less distraction?**

   Somewhat. The software uses drawing tools and recorded narration so it may distract, but it also has the ability to help students focus on what they are doing and why. It depends on how the teacher monitors the use and provides guided practice beforehand.

2. **Does the technology motivate students to start the learning process of knowledge gathering?**

   Yes. The software is very easy to use and may allow mathematical discourse to be more exciting and visible. The software makes it easier for students to explain their thinking because of the options of tools and ways to show their understanding.

3. **Does the technology cause a shift in the behavior of the students, where they go from being passive to active learners?**

   Somewhat. The software asks students to be hands-on by writing and narrating their mathematical solutions. While the teacher asks the students to do the activity individually, they are asked to narrate and explain their answers, so the activity does allow for a potential social feature. However joint engagement occurs, the teacher is monitoring comprehension only AFTER the recording.

Scenario 8

A ninth-grade English teacher studying memoirs and personal biographies asks each student to text message a six-word memoir and a short biography to an interactive website. The text messages are displayed anonymously on a website that the teacher projects.

Learning Goal: Students will understand the difference between a memoir and biography by sharing examples of their own.

1. **Does the technology allow students to focus on the assignment or activity with less distraction?**

   Somewhat. The software only has one way to respond and one question to respond to. However, since students have their cell phones out, they could become distracted. Management is key here.

2. **Does the technology motivate students to start the learning process of knowledge gathering?**

   Yes. The software uses cell phone technology, which the students are very comfortable with and allows everyone to participate quickly and immediately see their results on a digital board.

3. **Does the technology cause a shift in the behavior of the students, where they go from being passive to active social learners?**

   Somewhat. The software asks students to be hands-on by sending in their own responses. If the teacher also asked the students to "turn and talk" to discuss their answers or thoughts, it would provide the social piece that the activity is otherwise lacking.

Scenario 9

A fourth-grade teacher is using Google Hangouts to virtually host author Judy Blume conducting a book club discussion on her book *Tales of a Fourth Grade Nothing*. The students ask Judy questions and listen to her share ideas about writing and the novel.

Learning Goal: Have a discussion with Q&A for author Judy Blume about different aspects of her book (both content and writing style).

1. **Does the technology allow students to focus on the assignment or activity with less distraction?**

   Somewhat. The author being live is exciting, but the students could easily "zone out" if the conversation is not structured to the learners' levels or interests.

2. **Does the technology motivate students to start the learning process of knowledge gathering?**

   Yes. They can ask the author any question about her writing or the book.

3. **Does the technology cause a shift in the behavior of the students, where they go from being passive to active social learners?**

   Somewhat. The students are not hands-on with the technology, but there is a social aspect to the activity in that they are able to discuss ideas with the author via the technology tools.

Scenario 10

An 11th-grade science teacher is taking pictures of a class field trip to the chemistry museum and cutting them into a movie to show parents and students.

Learning Goal: Students will share what they learned about organic chemistry from their field trip to the chemistry museum.

1. **Does the technology allow students to focus on the assignment or activity with less distraction?**

    No. It actually may be more distracting for the students to watch the pictures being taken while they are working.

2. **Does the technology motivate students to start the learning process of knowledge gathering?**

    No. The students have no control or say in the technology and the way it is used.

3. **Does the technology cause a shift in the behavior of the students, where they go from being passive to active social learners?**

    No. The students are not hands-on with the technology nor are they co-constructing ideas through the technology tools.

Engagement Overview

In most of the above scenarios, the students are interacting with the technology tools on some level. They move into an active mode of learning by physically touching the device. If the activity is structured correctly (e.g., co-use and time-on-task), moving into a more active mode forces students to pay attention to the task at hand (rather than distracting from it) and ultimately focus on the learning goals. A couple of the scenarios have integrated a social aspect to the activity, sometimes with the technology (such as collaborating and editing together on a Google document) and sometimes around the technology (such as working in pairs using the technology). It is important that if co-engagement is not built into the tool, the teacher creates structures for co-use or joint-engagement around the technology tool. This co-use of the tools can lead to greater learning gains.

Engagement is a start. We want students to be focused, motivated, social, and hands-on learners, and technology can aid in creating this dynamic. However, technology can be more effective for learning by enhancing these learning experiences in ways that could not easily be done with traditional tools. In the next chapter we look at enhancement and how these same scenarios are measured through the level of enhancement.

Chapter Take-Aways

This chapter provided an overview of research in education that supports the need for technology to promote engagement, which creates active, social, and focused learners.

- Authentic engagement is social through co-use of a device or joint-engagement inside the digital media tool.

- Authentic engagement is active and time-on-task, meaning students focus on the learning process through the tool rather than being distracted from learning because of the digital tool.

- Authentic engagement can happen through the technology tool or around the technology tool with good instructional practices.

Chapter 5

Defining Enhancement

EDUCATORS OFTEN ASSERT that new or innovative technology tools enhance their students' learning. Yet, in reality it is unclear whether this assertion is true (Price & Kirkwood, 2010). One problem is that the term "enhancement" has not been clearly defined in its relation to education technology. Linda Price and Adrian Kirkwood (2010) describe the difficulty with defining the term as follows:

Technology-enhanced learning implies a value judgment: the word "enhancement" suggests an improvement or betterment some way. However, it is rare to find explicit statements about its meaning. How does technology enhance learning—what is the "value added?" Although there are many examples of innovative uses of technology in learning and teaching it is not clear whether these actually enhance student learning. More readily observed is the use of technology to support or replace existing teaching practices, with limited evidence to confirm any enhancements to the status quo. To date there has been an over-emphasis on technological manifestations and this has led to the omission of pedagogical considerations (Beetham, 2007; Conole et al., 2008; Kirkwood, 2009). (p.771)

Knowing that terms can easily be tossed around, it is important that enhancement of learning through technology tools has a measurable definition. This chapter highlights some practical ways to define the characteristics of enhancement when it comes to integrating technology tools with learning.

Adding Value

One essential aspect of measuring enhancement is focusing on the value added in content-specific learning goals. Many content-area experts agree that technology should move beyond engaging students in learning and actually change the learning experience so that it is improved over traditional methods (and not just an expensive substitution). One such example is the Technology Principle from the National Council for Teachers of Mathematics (NCTM) Principles and Standards for School Mathematics, which states, "Teachers should use technology to enhance their students' learning opportunities by selecting or creating mathematical tasks that take advantage of what technology can do efficiently and well—graphing, visualizing, and computing" (NCTM, 2000, p. 25). Price and Kirkwood (2014) found that "enhancement" could be defined under three types of improvement on traditional teaching methods: operational improvement (e.g., providing greater flexibility for students or making resources more accessible); quantitative change in learning (e.g., increased time-on-task or student improvement in test scores); and qualitative change in learning (e.g., promoting reflection on learning and practice or helping develop a richer understanding of content).

Experts in the four major content areas (social studies, ELA, math, and science) seem to agree that opportunities for *operational improvement* by building knowledge based on students' prior knowledge, skills, and interests is important for better comprehension of the content (NCSS, 2016; National Council of Science, 2007; Anthony & Walshaw, 2009; Duke & Pearson, 2002). Consequently, technology should support opportunities to leverage students' skills and interests into content learning. Examples of this would be integrating technology tools that help to either differentiate or personalize instruction to add value to learning. In addition, content experts call for integrating technology tools that allow students to develop a more sophisticated understanding of the content by eliciting higher-order thinking skills, such as inquiry and reflection (NCSS, 2016; National Council of Science, 2007; Anthony & Walshaw, 2009; Duke & Pearson, 2002). An example of this would be students testing their own scientific hypothesis by engaging with Google Earth's Timelapse and Layers features to analyze and gather evidence of what environmental change looks like over time and ask questions about why it is happening.

Scaffolds and Supports to Deepen Learning

Technology should create opportunities for students to move beyond engagement with content; that is, technology should somehow aid, assist, or scaffold students' learning in ways that improve on traditional methods. At this level, learning can become differentiated, personalized, and more relatable to the learner and the technology is helping students think more deeply about content with higher-cognitive skills.

The Triple E Framework defines enhancement as technology adding value to students' traditional understanding of learning goals through scaffolds or other supports. The technology or tool:

- supports students in *developing a more sophisticated understanding* of the content (higher-order thinking skills);

- creates ways *(scaffolds)* to make it easier to understand concepts or ideas;

- and creates paths for students to *demonstrate their understanding of the learning goals* in a way that they could not do with traditional tools.

A Look at Tools That Promote Enhancement

Table 5.1 lists possible instructional strategies to use when features of enhancement are organically part of the tool. One example is software that differentiates the same content based on reading levels to allow students to read the same content as their peers but at their "just right" reading level. Table 5.1 also lists strategies teachers can use to create enhancement around the use of the technology tool when enhancement is not present within the tool. For example, students working with a "drill and practice" piece of software could be given a checklist of higher-level probing questions to stop and ask each other as they work.

Table 5.1 Enhancement Take-Away Strategies

Characteristic of Enhancement	When Instructional Strategies for Enhancement Are Built into Tool	When Instructional Strategies for Enhancement Are NOT Built into Tool
Scaffolds to reach more sophisticated understanding through higher-order thinking	Opportunities exist for inquiry learning, to investigate an idea, collect data, and show understanding. Tool has built-in ways for students to reflect (and use higher-order thinking) on what they are doing on the device, not just consume knowledge.	Students participate in classroom discussions or turn-and-talks to construct hypotheses and new ideas from what they are learning through the tool. Students practice reflective thinking strategies and self-questioning. Tool allows visual representations of thinking (graphic organizer).

Characteristic of Enhancement	When Instructional Strategies for Enhancement Are Built into Tool	When Instructional Strategies for Enhancement Are NOT Built into Tool
Added value beyond traditional tools (differentiation and personalization)	The technology allows teachers to easily differentiate learning (e.g., assign students to reading level groups, allow students to get synchronized individual feedback based on their mathematical problem-solving). The technology allows teachers to personalize learning for each student's interests (e.g., students can choose to pursue a problem based on their interests, students can choose a way to share their knowledge based on their skills).	Teachers give students checklists or support sheets based on their learning level. Teachers assign students to work in similar interest teams around the technology. Students can select "just right" tools. Tool allows students a choice in how to represent their work.

Note: Strategies for "outside of the tool" are explained in detail in Chapter 9.

As mentioned in previous chapters, most educational technology is not built with educational experts or research in mind. However, there are some tools that promote enhancement. Table 5.2 includes a few examples of technology tools that have enhancement characteristics organically built into the tool.

Table 5.2 Technology Tools That Promote Enhancement

Name of Tool	Value-Added Supports or Scaffolds	Advantages over Traditional Tools	Content Area	Cost
Classkick & Formative	Both apps allow teachers to set up activities for students and synchronously watch and participate in learning activities with students. Activities can be set up based on student learning or interest levels.	Teachers can vary activities in the classroom for students based on learning levels, and they can watch and participate in real time as students are working.	ALL	Free

Continued

Name of Tool	Value-Added Supports or Scaffolds	Advantages over Traditional Tools	Content Area	Cost
Kaizena (kaizena.com)	Website provides synchronous editing and feedback between students and teachers, and allows real-time collaboration on documents, writing, and research. Feedback can be created via text, audio recording, video, and/ or links.	Feedback is real time so students can revise their work as they are involved in the writing process. Teachers can easily differentiate instruction and type of feedback with this tool.	ALL	Free
Imagistory	An early literacy app set up for children to co-construct a story with others based on images and audio.	Young children work together to build and record a story. They are able to easily listen to an audio recording of themselves telling their story aloud.	ELA	Free
Google My Maps	A mapping tool where students co-construct maps in real time. Students can work with others to add video, images, points of interest, and more to their interactive maps.	Students are able to easily co-construct a map that can be modi-fied or updated based on real events, people, or places. They also can share the map with others and edit anytime!	ALL	Free
TweenTribune (tweentribune.com)	Articles posted by the Smithsonian are differentiated based on students' reading Lexile levels.	The technology allows for easy differentiation of the same content.	ELA	Free

Scenarios of Enhancement

Here are three questions, developed as part of the Triple E Framework, to ask when measuring for enhancement of learning through technology tools.

1. Does the technology tool aid students in developing a more sophisticated understanding of the content (higher-order thinking skills)?

2. Does the technology create scaffolds to make it easier to understand concepts, gather information, or generate ideas?

3. Does the technology create paths for students to comprehend or demonstrate their understanding of the learning goals in a way that they could not do with traditional tools?

Using the three questions, consider if enhancement is present in each scenario.

Scenario 1

A second-grade teacher presenting a unit on ecosystems gives student pairs iPads that are preloaded with software for exploring various ecosystems in 3D. The software uses authentic images and live webcams from real ecosystems around the world, allowing students to click and tap on animals and plants in the ecosystems to learn more about them. The software also has a recorded notebook feature that lets students audio record oral observations, paste in images from the software, or type their scientific observations.

Learning Goal: Students will develop a hypothesis around what types of plants and animals live in different ecosystems and record their hypothesis with evidence to corroborate their thoughts.

1. **Does the technology tool aid students in developing a more sophisticated understanding of the content?**

   Yes. Since the software can explore authentic ecosystems as students tap and swipe on plants and animals, it allows them to personalize their learning experiences according to their interests in the ecosystems. They can also record and reflect (using higher-order thinking) on their observations based on live webcam feed.

2. **Does the technology create scaffolds to make it easier to understand concepts, gather information, or generate ideas?**

   Somewhat. Since the software allows students to explore authentic ecosystems as they tap and swipe on plants and animals (and view the live webcam), it provides them with a better understanding than what they might get from simply looking at a picture in a textbook. It would be even better if there were pre-defined probing questions built into recording pieces to support their reflective thinking.

3. **Does the technology create paths for students to comprehend or demonstrate their understanding of the learning goals in a way that they could not do with traditional ideas?**

   Somewhat. The scientific notebook feature allows students to record their observations in a way that is comfortable for them and possibly even copy, paste, and organize data. This could be done with more traditional pen/paper but would probably take longer and be less sophisticated in organization. The live webcams do allow students to observe authentic ecosystems rather than relying on videos or images.

Scenario 2

A teacher asks students to use math software on individual desktop computers. The software allows the teacher to program differentiated learning paths for each student so that when they log in, they are working in their individual zones of proximal development (ZPD). The software uses simulations and videos with short-answer explanations rather than "drill and practice" questions, and it lets the teacher provide immediate feedback (synchronously) as students take different assessments in a game-like format.

Learning Goal: Students will be able to show their understanding of how to calculate the surface area and perimeter of geometry shapes by participating in mathematical assessment of geometric figures.

1. **Does the technology tool aid students in developing a more sophisticated understanding of the content?**

   No. While the software can differentiate learning, the students are only using "drill and practice" skills and lower-order thinking. They are not being asked to use analysis, synthesis, creation, or other higher-order cognitive skills.

2. **Does the technology create scaffolds to make it easier to understand concepts, gather information, or generate ideas?**

   Somewhat. The software gives immediate feedback in the form of hints and tips on how to solve the problems, and it differentiates the learning for each student based on their ZPD. However, it would be different for students to generate their own ideas in this "drill and practice" software.

3. **Does the technology create paths for students to comprehend or demonstrate their understanding of the learning goals in a way that they could not do with traditional ideas?**

   Yes. It would be very difficult and time-consuming for a teacher to give immediate feedback in a classroom where students are all working on differentiated lessons in their ZPD.

Scenario 3

A social studies teacher is conducting a lecture by projecting a slideshow on static presentation software. The lecture is on visual inquiry, and the students are listening to and watching the presentation without technology in their hands; only the teacher is using technology.

Learning Goal: Students will understand how to do visual inquiry on images from the Revolutionary War time period. They will be able to understand the skill of visual inquiry and apply inquiry to any image.

1. **Does the technology tool aid students in developing a more sophisticated understanding of the content?**

   Somewhat. The presentation tools include sharing options for multimedia (such as images or videos) that could help students understand the content better than using a textbook. However, the students are not being asked to engage in higher-order thinking through the technology tools. The teacher could structure a discussion that elicits inquiry questions and reflections on the content.

2. **Does the technology create scaffolds to make it easier to understand concepts, gather information, or generate ideas?**

    Somewhat. The presentation tools include sharing options for multimedia (such as images or videos) that could help students understand the content better than using a textbook. But it would be difficult to differentiate or personalize content for each learner through one static slideshow.

3. **Does the technology create paths for students to comprehend or demonstrate their understanding of the learning goals in a way that they could not do with traditional ideas?**

    No. Students can take notes with paper and pencil during the lecture. But because they are not hands-on with the presentation technology, they cannot demonstrate their understanding in a nontraditional way.

Scenario 4

A kindergarten teacher focusing on early literacy goals of writing capital letters has each student come up to the interactive whiteboard to trace letters with the whiteboard pens.

Learning Goal: Students will be able to recognize letters and properly write capital letters.

1. **Does the technology tool aid students in developing a more sophisticated understanding of the content?**

    Somewhat. The whiteboard tool allows students to trace specific patterns of letters and watch others do it with potential feedback, but this could be done on a regular whiteboard or blackboard rather than an interactive whiteboard. Students are not being asked to engage in reflective or creative practices through the tool itself.

2. **Does the technology create scaffolds to make it easier to understand concepts, gather information, or generate ideas?**

    No. This could be done with paper and pencil or on a blackboard. If the teacher changed the tracing experience to meet each student's writing level, then that might better meet this learning target.

3. **Does the technology create paths for students to comprehend or demon-strate their understanding of the learning goals in a way that they could not do with traditional ideas?**

    No. This could be done with paper and pencil and may be better that way because a finger or marker is not as easy to use as a traditional pencil for students learning to write.

Scenario 5

A social studies and mathematics teacher has students working in pairs to use a website that is tracking the live primary election results. The students are posting their predictions into a Google Sheets collaborative spreadsheet to share what they think will happen in the next hours of voting based on the real-time voting results. The students then set up the spreadsheet equation editor to calculate how far off their predictions were as the live results come in.

Learning Goal: Students will be able to understand how to make predictions in mathematics.

1. **Does the technology tool aid students in developing a more sophisticated understanding of the content?**

    Yes. Because the website is real time, they can see immediately how the results are changing minute by minute. In addition, they are asked to use the numbers to create math expressions for prediction. Thus, there are higher-order thinking skills occurring through the tools.

2. **Does the technology create scaffolds to make it easier to understand concepts, gather information, or generate ideas?**

    Yes. The website gives authentic and immediate results, which allows students to see results in real time. It also allows students to personalize their predictions by selecting particular candidates to follow or counties for results.

3. **Does the technology create paths for students to comprehend or demon-strate their understanding of the learning goals in a way that they could not do with traditional ideas?**

    Yes. It would be almost impossible for students to track real-time election results without the technology tools.

Scenario 6

An English teacher asks students to use a static ebook app on their iPads that explains how to write a five-paragraph essay. Each student has his or her own iPad and swipes through after reading each page. When students finish, they get their name on top of a leaderboard if they finish reading in under 15 minutes. Then the students start working on their five-paragraph essay (using pen and paper).

Learning Goal: Students will learn how to write a five-paragraph essay.

1. **Does the technology tool aid students in developing a more sophisticated understanding of the content?**

   No. The ebook is not interactive, it's just a story, so students could have learned the same from the teacher lecturing. It is also easy for the students to skip content by swiping through quickly without reading. Since it is timed, students are likely to swipe quickly so they can get to the top of the leaderboard, but this often means content may be missed. Students are not being asked to use higher-cognitive skills through the tool.

2. **Does the technology create scaffolds to make it easier to understand concepts, gather information, or generate ideas?**

   No. Because the content is static and not "clickable," it may actually be more useful if the students learned from their teacher and saw examples while pausing for questions.

3. **Does the technology create paths for students to comprehend or demonstrate their understanding of the learning goals in a way that they could not do with traditional ideas?**

   No. The teacher could easily lecture about a five-paragraph essay and do checks for understanding face to face.

Scenario 7

A fifth-grade teacher focusing on multiplying fractions asks students to each use interactive screencasting software on an iPad to show how they solve a problem. Students can record their own screens as they solve the math problem, and they can use the text and drawing tools simultaneously to show their mathematical thinking behind each step. The recording is sent to the teacher.

Learning Goal: Students will understand how to multiply fractions and show their work.

1. **Does the technology tool aid students in developing a more sophisticated understanding of the content?**

   Yes. It allows students to create, show, and talk through their mathematical solutions while their work is recorded for the teacher to see and evaluate. The tool asks students to use higher-order thinking skills. They can also re-record.

2. **Does the technology create scaffolds to make it easier to understand concepts, gather information, or generate ideas?**

   Somewhat. The software is not set up to make things easier or to differentiate for mathematics, but students do have a variety of drawing tools to choose from to demonstrate what they know.

3. **Does the technology create paths for students to comprehend or demonstrate their understanding of the learning goals in a way that they could not do with traditional ideas?**

   Yes. It would be very difficult to do this with traditional tools and record student thinking in this way. In addition, it would also be time-consuming for the teacher to individually sit down with each student and ask about their mathematical thinking.

Scenario 8

A ninth-grade English teacher studying memoirs and personal biographies asks each student to text message a six-word memoir and a short biography to an interactive website. The text messages are displayed anonymously on a website that the teacher projects.

Learning Goal: Students will understand the difference between a memoir and biography by sharing examples of their own.

1. **Does the technology tool aid students in developing a more sophisticated understanding of the content?**

   No. Students are just sharing their memoirs.

2. **Does the technology create scaffolds to make it easier to understand concepts, gather information, or generate ideas?**

   Somewhat. The technology makes it easier to share all the memoirs at once and archive them, but it does not differentiate for individual learners. Students can personalize their memoirs.

3. **Does the technology create paths for students to comprehend or demonstrate their understanding of the learning goals in a way that they could not do with traditional ideas?**

   Somewhat. It allows students to share anonymously and all at once, which would be more difficult with paper and pencil or even a chalkboard share out. However, students could write and share six-word memoirs without the aid of the technology.

Scenario 9

A fourth-grade teacher is using Google Hangouts to virtually host author Judy Blume conducting a book club discussion on her book *Tales of a Fourth Grade Nothing*. The students ask Judy questions and listen to her share ideas about writing and the novel.

Learning Goal: Have a discussion with Q&A for author Judy Blume about different aspects of her book (both content and writing style).

1. **Does the technology tool aid students in developing a more sophisticated understanding of the content?**

   Somewhat. They can talk directly to the author, get questions answered, and reflect as a group with the author. While they could write letters back and forth, the technology creates the opportunity for synchronous inquiry questioning, reflection, and feedback.

2. **Does the technology create scaffolds to make it easier to understand concepts, gather information, or generate ideas?**

   Somewhat. It allows the students to talk directly to the author in order to gather their information rather than having to search the internet or other secondary resources. There is some limited personalization in which students can ask questions based on their own interests.

3. **Does the technology create paths for students to comprehend or demonstrate their understanding of the learning goals in a way that they could not do with traditional ideas?**

   Yes. There is a very slim chance that an author would come to their school. A virtual live meeting is something that can only happen with the technology.

Scenario 10

An 11th-grade science teacher is taking pictures of a class field trip to the chemistry museum and cutting them into a movie to show to parents and students.

Learning Goal: Students will share what they learned about organic chemistry from their field trip to the chemistry museum.

1. **Does the technology tool aid students in developing a more sophisticated understanding of the content?**

   No. The teacher is doing all the work with the technology.

2. **Does the technology create scaffolds to make it easier to understand concepts, gather information, or generate ideas**

   No. The teacher is using the technology to document the learning.

3. **Does the technology create paths for students to comprehend or demonstrate their understanding of the learning goals in a way that they could not do with traditional ideas?**

   No. The students are not engaged with the technology in a way that they are directly learning through it.

Enhancement Overview

Most of these scenarios had some level of engagement (as described in Chapter 4). Yet notice how some of the teaching scenarios that had engagement did not necessarily have the characteristics of enhancement. At the enhancement target, we are looking for "value added" to the learning goals. Thus, students could be engaged in time-on-task using an app, but not learning more than if they were using a traditional workbook. For example, the kindergarten teacher's lesson using the interactive whiteboard for literacy learning can be fun and perhaps engaging to students, but the interactive whiteboard is not doing anything to enhance a student's understanding of the learning goals that traditional tools could not do. A teacher could easily use a whiteboard and post outlines of letters for students to trace, or use paper and pencil and have the same desired results. Other scenarios are enhancing the learning goals by adding opportunities for students to engage in higher-order thinking skills, differentiating learning, or providing learning opportunities that traditional tools could not easily offer.

The next chapter will explore the final component of the framework: extension. Once again, these same scenarios will be presented through the lens of how well the learning goals are extended to everyday life through the technology tools.

Chapter Take-Aways

This chapter provided an overview of enhancement, one of the components of the Triple E Framework, offering practical ways to enable students to engage in higher-order thinking skills and access deeper learning opportunities than traditional tools typically can.

- Authentic enhancement is a value added to learning experiences.

- Authentic enhancement should help to elicit higher-order thinking skills.

- Authentic enhancement should help to differentiate learning.

- Authentic enhancement should help to personalize learning.

- Authentic enhancement should provide supports that traditional tools cannot easily provide.

Chapter 6

Defining Extension

LEARNING DOES NOT take place in isolation. Educators often describe the importance of bridging classroom learning with everyday life. Jerome Bruner (1966) describes this bridge: "What we resolve to do in school only makes sense when considered in the broader context of what the society intends to accomplish through its educational investment in the young" (Preface ix). Educators tend to agree that cognition should not be separated or isolated from its context (Brown, Collins & Duguid, 1989). Learning happens best when it is situated in culture, language, context, and time. According to Darling-Hammond et al. (2008), students learn more deeply when they can apply classroom content learning to real-world problems. Using emerging technologies is one way to help create these authentic connections (Harrington et al., 2010). Finding ways to situate learning in its natural environment is a fundamental piece of developing lessons.

Furthermore, according to a National Education Association Policy Brief (2008), for many students, what happens before and after school can be as important as what happens during the school day. High-quality extended learning enriches opportunities for students by complementing school learning. Expanding students' opportunities to connect their academic learning with their community helps students to develop non-academic skills and to sustain motivation and persistence in achieving their academic learning goals (Halpern, 2012).

Authenticity Is Key

In 1897, John Dewey argued, "Education is not preparation for life, education is life itself." Learning experiences should bridge students' current everyday life and classroom experiences. If technology can aid in the ability to create these real-world connections, then learning is being extended outside of the classroom walls and into students' everyday lives.

Content area experts have found that authenticity in lessons is linked to student learning gains (NCSS, 2016; National Council of Science, 2007; Anthony & Walshaw, 2009). While there is much focus on future skills, it is important to remember that we are not certain which future skills students may need; thus a priority of learning is to make authentic connections to students' current lives, rather than figure out how skills and knowledge will fit into their future 20 years from today. If students can use technology to extend their learning experiences to make sense of the world around them, ultimately they will gain better comprehension of the learning goals.

In addition to addressing students' current lives, The Partnership for 21st Century Skills (2011) developed a framework that describes the skills and knowledge students should master in order to succeed in the current workforce. Their framework asserts that for children to be successful in the workplace, they must learn the skills of the current workforce in schools (not necessarily the future workforce). There are three digital age skills outside of the core subjects that the Partnership for 21st Century Skills recommends be part of student outcomes in schools. First, students should develop learning and innovation skills such as critical thinking, communication, creativity, and collaboration. We have already touched on the idea of using these higher-level thinking skills as part of enhancement. Second, students should develop information, media, and technology skills so they can quickly adapt to new tools and use current tools for information gathering, dissemination, and collaborating with others. Third, students need to develop life and career skills such as the ability to adapt to change, take initiative, work effectively across diverse groups, manage projects, and produce effective results. These are some of the "soft" skills that will help students better navigate their everyday lives.

Table 6.1 lists possible instructional strategies to use when extension features are organically built into the tool. An example is software that allows students studying polar bears to synchronously connect with expert scientists in Canada doing fieldwork with polar bears. Table 6.1 also lists strategies teachers can use to create extension around the use of the technology tool when extension is not present within the tool. For example, students working on an Excel spreadsheet to learn about linear and non-linear graphs could gather data for the graph from their own life experiences.

Table 6.1 Extension Take-Away Strategies

Characteristic of Extension	When Instructional Strategies for Extension Are Built into Tool	When Instructional Strategies for Extension Are NOT Built into Tool
Allows students to learn 24/7	Students can continue to collect data, reflect, and research through the tool easily outside of school (e.g., a mobile device that allows students to record interviews on-the-go).	Students use analog resources and methods to collect data and then use their technology tool back in the classroom.
Bridges everyday experiences with school learning	Use technology to synchronously connect with students or experts in another location. Use technology to help solve real-world problems.	Ask students to go out into their community and look for connections to the learning, then report back to class via oral or written work. Use tech-to-self connections. Create an authentic context.
Everyday soft skills	Technology helps students manage tasks, communicate, and collaborate with others, while expertly gathering knowledge about the world around them.	Practice modeling the soft skills in person, and then try them via the technology tools.

Note: Strategies for "outside of the tool" are explained in detail in Chapter 9.

A Look at Tools That Promote Extension

While teachers often need to create authentic contexts around technology tools, there are some tools that make it easier to connect to everyday life because they are built for these connections. Table 6.2 includes a few examples of technology tools that organically have extension characteristics built into the tool.

Table 6.2 Tools That Promote Extension

Name of Tool	Connection to Everyday Life	Content Area	Cost
The WildLab (thewildlab.org)	Students are invited to collect and share images and descriptions of birds in their local area in this collaborative website.	Science and Social Studies	Free
SepiaTown (sepiatown.com)	Students are invited to locate and share vintage photos from their local area on this collaborative website.	Social Studies	Free
Figment (figment.com)	Students are invited to write stories, provide feedback on stories (feedback is moderated!), and share their writing with a national audience. This is a positive community to share and collaborate with on writing.	ELA	Free
GooseChase (goosechase.com)	Teachers (or students) can set up mobile scavenger hunts around their community (or on a field trip). Students can participate in the hunts alone or with a team, documenting their hunt with images, video, and text submissions.	ALL	Free or Premium
Klikaklu (klikaklu.com)	Teachers (or students) can create photo scavenger hunts around the local community (or on field trips). Students can participate in the hunts via their mobile phones and share results through the app.	ALL	Free or Premium

Continued

Name of Tool	Connection to Everyday Life	Content Area	Cost
Lab4U (lab4u.co)	Students can download the science lab apps (chemistry, physics, and biology) to their mobile devices and use the apps to conduct real-time experiments wherever they are!	Science	Free
Google Hangouts Twitter Skype	Students can use tools like Google Hangouts, Twitter, or Skype to connect with experts, other classrooms, and leaders in educational fields.	ALL	Free

Scenarios of Extension

Here are three questions, developed as part of the Triple E Framework, to ask when measuring for extension of learning through technology tools.

1. Does the technology create opportunities for students to learn outside of their typical school day?

2. Does the technology create a bridge between school learning and everyday life experiences?

3. Does the technology allow students to build skills that they can use in their everyday lives?

Using the three questions, consider if extension is present in the following scenarios.

Scenario 1

A second-grade teacher presenting a unit on ecosystems gives student pairs iPads that are preloaded with software for exploring various ecosystems in 3D. The software uses authentic images and live webcams from real ecosystems around the world, allowing students to click and tap on animals and plants in the ecosystems to learn more about them. The software also has a recorded notebook feature that lets students audio record oral observations, paste in images from the software, or type their scientific observations.

Learning Goal: Students will develop a hypothesis around what types of plants and animals live in different ecosystems and record their hypothesis with evidence to corroborate their thoughts.

1. **Does the technology create opportunities for students to learn outside of their typical school day?**

    Somewhat. They are only possible if they have the software at home.

2. **Does the technology create a bridge between school learning and everyday life experiences?**

    Yes. By using authentic images and videos, the software allows students to access ecosystems that they would not be able to access through more traditional means.

3. **Does the technology allow students to develop skills that they can use in their everyday lives?**

    Somewhat. They are learning how to build a scientific notebook and observational skills, but they are not connecting skills directly to their everyday culture or habitat.

Scenario 2

A teacher asks students to use math software on individual desktop computers. The software allows the teacher to program differentiated learning paths for each student so that when they log in, they are working in their individual zones of proximal development (ZPD). The software uses simulations and videos with short-answer explanations rather than "drill and practice" questions, and it allows the teacher to provide immediate feedback (synchronously) as students take different assessments in a game-like format.

Learning Goal: Students will be able to show their understanding of how to calculate the surface area and perimeter of geometry shapes by participating in mathematical assessment of geometric figures.

1. **Does the technology create opportunities for students to learn outside of their typical school day?**

    No. Most likely students do not own the software. Teachers would also need to be online at the same time, which is unlikely.

2. **Does the technology create a bridge between school learning and everyday life experiences?**

   No. The software has activities that are not based on authentic experiences, thus the students are not likely to easily see connections to their own cultural experiences and math.

3. **Does the technology allow students to develop skills that they can use in their everyday lives?**

   No. Though they are learning mathematics, the skills are very specific to the highly technical goals of Common Core State Standards for Mathematics.

Scenario 3

A social studies teacher is conducting a lecture by projecting a slideshow on static presentation software. The lecture is on visual inquiry, and the students are listening to and watching the presentation without technology in their hands; only the teacher is using technology.

Learning Goal: Students will understand how to do visual inquiry on images from the Revolutionary War time period. They will be able to understand the skill of visual inquiry and apply inquiry to any image.

1. **Does the technology create opportunities for students to learn outside of their typical school day?**

   No. Unless they have access to the slideshow and teacher lecturing at home, students would not be able to take the lecture with them.

2. **Does the technology create a bridge between school learning and everyday life experiences?**

   No. While the lecture could incorporate images from students' everyday lives, in general there are not these type of connections.

3. **Does the technology allow students to develop skills that they can use in their everyday lives?**

   No. Watching a slideshow and listening to a lecture does not directly connect them to new technology or cultural skills.

Scenario 4

A kindergarten teacher focusing on early literacy goals of writing capital letters has each student come up to the interactive whiteboard to trace letters with the whiteboard pens.

Learning Goal: Students will be able to recognize letters and properly write capital letters.

1. **Does the technology create opportunities for students to learn outside of their typical school day?**

   No. The interactive whiteboard is not an option for students to use outside of school.

2. **Does the technology create a bridge between school learning and everyday life experiences?**

   No. The students would be able to see the connections between the letters and their everyday literacy life, but the technology has little to do with it. They could do so without the technology tool.

3. **Does the technology allow students to develop skills that they can use in their everyday lives?**

   No. No soft skills are being brought into this activity through the technology tools.

Scenario 5

A social studies and mathematics teacher has students working in pairs to use a website that is tracking the live primary election results. The students are posting their predictions into a Google Sheets collaborative spreadsheet to share what they think will happen in the next hours of voting based on the real-time voting results. The students then set up the spreadsheet equation editor to calculate how far off their predictions were as the live results come in.

Learning Goal: Students will be able to understand how to make predictions in mathematics.

1. **Does the technology create opportunities for students to learn outside of their typical school day?**

    Yes. The students can learn how to use real-time data and websites to make predictions.

2. **Does the technology create a bridge between school learning and everyday life experiences?**

    Yes. By using the website with authentic data, students are able to create connections to everyday life around elections and the electoral process in their local news.

3. **Does the technology allow students to develop skills that they can use in their everyday lives?**

    Somewhat. Students are learning how to interpret authentic data to manipulate and make predictions. They are gaining some soft skills around managing data, but more could be done with other soft skills.

Scenario 6

An English teacher asks students to use a static ebook app on their iPads that explains how to write a five-paragraph essay. Each student has his or her own iPad and swipes through after reading each page. When students finish, they get their name on top of a leaderboard if they finish reading in under 15 minutes. Then the students start working on their five-paragraph essay (using pen and paper).

Learning Goal: Students will learn how to write a five-paragraph essay.

1. **Does the technology create opportunities for students to learn outside of their typical school day?**

    No. The content of the ebook is focused heavily on writing a formal essay, and students are not likely to use it in their everyday lives.

2. **Does the technology create a bridge between school learning and everyday life experiences?**

    No. The technology does not include content related to the everyday cultural lives of students; the content is generic.

3. **Does the technology allow students to develop skills that they can use in their everyday lives?**

    Somewhat. If students need to learn about formal essay writing, it possibly could help.

Scenario 7

A fifth-grade teacher focusing on multiplying fractions asks students to each use interactive screencasting software on an iPad to show how they solve a problem. Students can record their own screens as they solve the math problem, and they can use the text and drawing tools simultaneously to show their mathematical thinking behind each step. The recording is sent to the teacher.

Learning Goal: Students will understand how to multiply fractions and show their work.

1. **Does the technology create opportunities for students to learn outside of their typical school day?**

    Somewhat. Opportunities are only possible if they have the software and devices at home.

2. **Does the technology create a bridge between school learning and everyday life experiences?**

    No. The problem-solving tasks are not authentic situations.

3. **Does the technology allow students to develop skills that they can use in their everyday lives?**

    Somewhat. They are learning to talk through their ideas with the aid of the technology, but more could be done to connect soft skills to experiences in authentic situations.

Scenario 8

A ninth-grade English teacher studying memoirs and personal biographies asks each student to text message a six-word memoir and a short biography to an interactive website. The text messages are displayed anonymously on a website that the teacher projects.

Learning Goal: Students will understand the difference between a memoir and biography by sharing examples of their own.

1. **Does the technology create opportunities for students to learn outside of their typical school day?**

    Somewhat. By incorporating technology tools that the students use in their everyday lives, the lesson helps students use the tool as a learning device.

2. **Does the technology create a bridge between school learning and everyday life experiences?**

    No. The content, while personal, is still isolated to the classroom.

3. **Does the technology allow students to develop skills that they can use in their everyday lives?**

    No. While they are sharing their memoirs, students are not required to write biographies on their cell phones as an everyday skill.

Scenario 9

A fourth-grade teacher is using Google Hangouts to virtually host author Judy Blume conducting a book club discussion on her book *Tales of a Fourth Grade Nothing*. The students ask Judy questions and listen to her share ideas about writing and the novel.

Learning Goal: Have a discussion with Q&A for author Judy Blume about different aspects of her book (both content and writing style).

1. **Does the technology create opportunities for students to learn outside of their typical school day?**

    Yes. By using a common and free tool to bring in an expert, students are able to connect with experts at any point in time.

2. **Does the technology create a bridge between school learning and everyday life experiences?**

    Yes. Bringing in a real author via virtual means is almost as good as the real thing!

3. **Does the technology allow students to develop skills that they can use in their everyday lives?**

    Somewhat. While they do see how to connect with others from a distance, they are not actually using the tools themselves to do this, their teacher is. At the same time, they are learning how to engage in dialogue in a virtual webinar.

Scenario 10

An 11th-grade science teacher is taking pictures of a class field trip to the chemistry museum and cutting them into a movie to show to parents and students.

Learning Goal: Students will share what they learned about organic chemistry from their field trip to the chemistry museum.

1. **Does the technology create opportunities for students to learn outside of their typical school day?**

    No. The students are not learning how to use the technology or learning through the technology.

2. **Does the technology create a bridge between school learning and everyday life experiences?**

    Somewhat. The images reflect the students' experience, but students do not learn how to use the technology to document their learning.

3. **Does the technology allow students to develop skills that they can use in their everyday lives?**

    No. The students are not using the technology.

Extension Overview

As in the three previous chapters, notice that while there may have been engagement and/or enhancement in the scenarios, some activities were lacking the connection to authentic experiences through the technology tools. Consequently, a piece of software or tool may help to add value and create co-use around learning goals, but it still might not connect students' classroom learning to their everyday lives. While all three levels do not have to be met, aiming to meet each Triple E component is the goal!

The next chapter will explore the tool used to measure the Triple E Framework, and once again we will examine these scenarios to see how well each scores on the measurement tool.

Chapter Take-Aways

This chapter demonstrated how technology should create opportunities for students to move beyond engagement in content, to a level where their learning can become differentiated, personalized, and more relatable.

- Authentic extension should involve real connections to everyday life contexts and tasks.

- Authentic extension should be a bridge between student learning and students' lives.

- Authentic extension should build skills for everyday living.

Chapter 7

The Triple E Measurement Tool

THIS CHAPTER COVERS the Triple E Framework measurement tool, which was developed as a guide for educators integrating technology into their lesson plans. The measurement tool explores each component of the framework by asking educators to answer three questions at each Triple E level. Each question earns a score of 0, 1, or 2. The score is 0 if the criteria are not present in the lesson; the score is 1 if the criteria are somewhat present in the lesson; the score is 2 if the criteria are absolutely present in the lesson. After all the questions have been answered, the score is totaled. The final total can be anywhere from 0 to 18.

Using the Measurement Tool

The nine-item Triple E measurement tool is below. An interactive measurement tool can be found at the Triple E Framework website (tripleeframework.com).

Engagement in the Learning	0=No	1=Somewhat	2=Yes
The technology allows students to focus on the assignment or activity with less distraction. (time-on-task)			
The technology motivates students to start the learning process.			
The technology causes a shift in the behavior of the students, where they move from passive to active social learners. (co-use)			
Enhancement of the Learning Goals	0=No	1=Somewhat	2=Yes
The technology tool allows students to develop a more sophisticated understanding of the learning goals or content. (higher-order thinking skills)			
The technology creates supports (scaffolds) to make it easier to understand concepts or ideas.			
The technology creates paths for students to demonstrate their understanding of the learning goals in a way that they could not do with traditional tools.			
Extension of the Learning Goals	0=No	1=Somewhat	2=Yes
The technology creates opportunities for students to learn outside of their typical school day.			
The technology creates a bridge between students' school learning and their everyday life experiences.			
The technology allows students to develop skills that they can use in their everyday lives.			

Reading Results

Below are the suggested result groupings and advice for understanding point totals. These are by no means concrete; rather the results should be considered a guide for teachers to think about the usefulness of their pedagogical choices with the technology tools in their lesson. As with everything in education, interpretation is key, thus there may be some variation on how each teacher interprets each level.

Key to point totals

13–18 Points *(Green Light)*. When a lesson has at least 13 points, it is always meeting all three components of the Framework. Therefore, these lessons tend to show a remarkable connection between the technology tools, instructional choices around the tool, and students' focus and comprehension of the learning goals. Students should be engaged as active time-on-task social learners through the technology. Students' understanding of the learning goals should be enhanced through the technology in ways that traditional tools could not easily do, and finally, students' understanding of the learning goals should transcend the classroom so that they are connecting what they are learning to their everyday lives.

7–12 Points *(Yellow Light)*. When a lesson receives between 10 and 12 points, it is meeting at least two of the three levels of the Framework. By meeting at least two levels (most often engagement and enhancement, or engagement and extension), there is a strong connection between technology tools and students' comprehension of the learning goals. When a lesson has between 7 and 9 points, the lesson is still meeting at least two levels of the Framework. However, it is not usually meeting the components at all the highest options. Thus, while there is a connection between technology and learning goals, educators should take time to re-evaluate the lesson and technology choices and instructional moves to make certain that technology enhances and/or extends the learning goals in some significant way. This may be an opportunity to add more instructional moves into the lesson to better leverage the technology for student learning.

6 Points or below *(Red Light)*. When a lesson has 6 points or below, the lesson is often meeting only one level of the Framework. This level is almost always engagement. Consequently, the connection between technology, instructional moves, and learning goals tends to be low. And if engagement is the only connection, the educators should reconsider whether this particular technology should be used in the lesson, if more instructional moves should be added to better leverage the technology for enhancing or extending learning, or if a more traditional method (not using technology) may be more appropriate. In particular, since technology tends to extol much time and energy to set up and implement, it should be used carefully and purposefully.

Revisiting Scenarios

In order to practice with the measurement tool, we will revisit the scenarios from the three previous chapters and look at the total score. In this section, I show the total points in each of the three Triple E measures as well as a final total with a short explanation of how to read the final total. The estimated time it took teachers to set up the technology (or complete the project with technology) is included. The reason for including this piece is to see if the end goals justify the amount of time the teacher had to spend preparing and finalizing the activity.

Scenario 1

A second-grade teacher presenting a unit on ecosystems gives student pairs iPads preloaded with software for exploring various ecosystems in 3D. The software uses authentic images and live webcams from real ecosystems around the world, allowing students to click and tap on animals and plants in the ecosystems to learn more about them. The software also has a recorded notebook feature that lets students audio record oral observations, paste in images from the software, or type their scientific observations.

Learning Goal: Students will develop a hypothesis around what types of plants and animals live in different ecosystems and record their hypothesis with evidence to corroborate their thoughts.

Setup Time: 15 minutes

Engagement	Enhancement	Extension	Total
6 points	4 points	3 points	13 points *(Green Light)*

Scoring Explanation: In this scenario, the technology has strong engagement because of the synchronous interactions between student and teacher as well as the active, time-on-task focus of the software. There is some enhancement by personalizing learning and asking students to reflect using higher-order thinking. The use of the webcams adds some authenticity that would be difficult to reach without the webcams.

Scenario 2

A teacher asks students to use math software on individual desktop computers. The software allows the teacher to program differentiated learning paths for each student so that when they log in, they are working in their individual zones of proximal development (ZPD). The software uses simulations and videos with short-answer explanations rather than "drill and practice" questions, and it allows the teacher to provide immediate feedback (synchronously) as students take different assessments in a game-like format.

Learning Goal: *Students will be able to show their understanding of how to calculate the surface area and perimeter of geometry shapes by participating in mathematical assessment of geometric figures.*

Setup Time: 20 minutes

Engagement	Enhancement	Extension	Total
6 points	4 points	0 points	10 points *(Yellow Light)*

Scoring Explanation: While the software is "drill and practice" (lower-cognitive thinking) and has no authentic connections to the students' everyday lives, the teacher can differentiate the learning levels and co-construct knowledge by giving students feedback as they work.

Scenario 3

A social studies teacher is conducting a lecture by projecting a slideshow on static presentation software. The lecture is on visual inquiry, and the students are listening to and watching the presentation without technology in their hands; only the teacher is using technology.

Learning Goal: *Students will understand how to do visual inquiry on images from the Revolutionary War time period. They will be able to understand the skill of visual inquiry and apply inquiry to any image.*

Setup Time: 2 hours

Engagement	Enhancement	Extension	Total
1 point	2 points	0 points	3 points *(Red Light)*

Scoring Explanation: The teacher should rethink how and why the technology is being used in this lesson. There is little engagement and little enhancement occurring and a lot of setup time involved in this project. Is there a better option?

Scenario 4

A kindergarten teacher focusing on early literacy goals has each student come up to the interactive whiteboard to trace letters with the whiteboard pens.

Learning Goal: *Students will be able to recognize letters and create them.*

Setup Time: 45 minutes

Engagement	Enhancement	Extension	Total
5 points	1 point	0 points	6 points *(Red Light)*

Scoring Explanation: This is a fun activity but includes very little enhancement or extension happening in the lesson. The teacher may want to consider modifying the lesson so that it would better differentiate or personalize learning as well as connect learning to students' everyday lives.

Scenario 5

A social studies and mathematics teacher has students working in pairs to use a website that is tracking the live primary election results. The students are posting their predictions into a Google Sheets collaborative spreadsheet to share what they think will happen in the next hours of voting based on the real-time voting results. The students then set up the spreadsheet equation editor to calculate how far off their predictions were as the live results come in.

Learning Goal: *Students will understand how to make predictions in mathematics.*

Setup Time: 5 minutes

Engagement	Enhancement	Extension	Total
6 points	6 points	5 points	17 points *(Green Light)*

Scoring Explanation: This is an exemplary lesson that wisely integrates technology in a way that co-engages students in learning how to make predictions and calculate live data while reflecting on their work with other students. The technology allows opportunities to add value to students' learning by having them use higher-order thinking around the data and requiring them to create calculations.

Scenario 6

An English teacher asks students to use a static ebook app on their iPads that explains how to write a five-paragraph essay. Each student has his or her own iPad and swipes through after reading each page. When students finish, they get their name on top of a leaderboard if they finish reading in under 15 minutes. Then the students start working on their five-paragraph essay (using pen and paper).

Learning Goal: *Students will learn how to write a five-paragraph essay.*

Setup Time: 30 minutes

Engagement	Enhancement	Extension	Total
2 points	0 points	1 point	3 points (Red Light)

Scoring Explanation: This lesson could easily be done without the technology. The ebook is providing very few benefits compared to a more traditional option. There is no collaboration or active hands-on learning. In addition, there are no higher-order thinking skills or authentic learning experiences that the technology tools are bringing into the lesson.

Scenario 7

A fifth-grade teacher focusing on multiplying fractions asks students to each use interactive screencasting software on an iPad to show how they solve a problem. Students can record their own screens as they solve the math problem, and they can use the text and drawing tools simultaneously to show their mathematical thinking behind each step. The recording is sent to the teacher.

Learning Goal: *Students will understand how to multiply fractions and show their work.*

Setup Time: 10 minutes

Engagement	Enhancement	Extension	Total
5 points	5 points	2 points	12 points (Yellow Light)

Scoring Explanation: This is a solid lesson with technology tools, meeting parts of each Triple E component. While the authentic connections are minimal, it has strong engagement and enhancement features. It asks the students to use higher-order thinking as they make their thought process visible, it actively engages them in the task of doing mathematics, and it allows the teacher to assess their learning and thinking.

Scenario 8

A ninth-grade English teacher studying memoirs and personal biographies asks each student to text message a six-word memoir and a short biography to an interactive website. The text messages are displayed anonymously on a website that the teacher projects.

Learning Goal: Students will understand the difference between a memoir and biography by sharing examples of their own.

Setup Time: 5 minutes

Engagement	Enhancement	Extension	Total
5 points	2 points	1 point	8 points *(Yellow Light)*

Scoring Explanation: This is a fun activity allowing students to take out their cell phones and text. However, the enhancement connections are minimal, and it may be wise for the teacher to modify the lesson or use a different tool to better add value to the learning goals.

Scenario 9

A fourth-grade teacher is using Google Hangouts to virtually host author Judy Blume conducting a book club discussion on her book *Tales of a Fourth Grade Nothing*. The students ask Judy questions and listen to her share ideas about writing and the novel.

Learning Goal: Have a discussion with Q&A for author Judy Blume about different aspects of her book (both content and writing style).

Setup Time: 5 minutes

Engagement	Enhancement	Extension	Total
4 points	5 points	5 points	14 points *(Green Light)*

Scoring Explanation: There is a lot of authenticity built into this lesson plan. Without the technology, it would be difficult to hold a synchronous conversation and book discussion with an expert author. The lesson also demonstrates how students can connect with experts and converse with them via web conferencing tools.

Scenario 10

An 11th-grade science teacher is taking pictures of a class field trip to the chemistry museum and cutting them into a movie to show to parents and students.

Learning Goal: Students will share what they learned about organic chemistry from their field trip to the chemistry museum.

Setup Time: 3 hours

Engagement	Enhancement	Extension	Total
0 points	0 points	1 point	1 point *(Red Light)*

Scoring Explanation: This lesson is teacher-centered, not hands-on for the students, and lacks any added value for the students' own learning.

Chapter Take-Aways

This chapter covered the Triple E Framework measurement tool, which is designed to help educators integrate technology into their lesson plans.

- When a lesson scores at least 13 points, it is meeting all three components of the Framework. This means the lesson bears a strong connection between the technology tools, instructional choices around the tool, and students' focus and comprehension of the learning goals.

- When a lesson receives between 10 and 12 points, it is meeting at least two of the three levels of the Framework. Thus, there is a strong connection between technology tools and students' comprehension of the learning goals.

- When a lesson receives between 7 and 9 points, it is not meeting the components at all the highest options. Thus, educators should re-evaluate the lesson and technology choices to ensure that technology enhances and/ or extends the learning goals in some significant way.

- When a lesson receives 6 points or fewer, it is often meeting only one level of the Framework—most often engagement. This indicates that the educator should reconsider if this particular technology should be used in the lesson, if the technology can be leveraged for enhancing or extending learning, or if a more traditional method may be more appropriate.

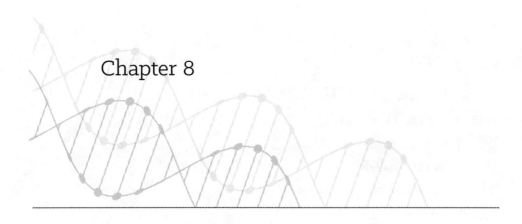

Chapter 8

Examples
from the Field

THIS CHAPTER EXPLORES authentic projects that meet all three areas of the Triple E Framework as well as the 2016 ISTE Standards for Students. The following projects and descriptions are contributions from the K–12 teachers who designed and taught the lessons. At the end of each project is a table showing how the lesson met the Triple E Framework.

Case Study 1
Scavenger Hunting for French Cultural Connections

Program Information

GRADE LEVEL: Kindergarten–Grade 2

SUBJECT AREA: French

TEACHER AND LESSON AUTHOR: Alyssa Marcangelo, Elementary French Teacher, Detroit County Day Lower School

LOCATION: Bloomfield Hills, Michigan

ISTE STANDARDS: Empowered Learner, Knowledge Constructor, Creative Communicator, Global Collaborator

LEARNING GOALS/STANDARDS MET

- To "immerse" students in a foreign culture;
- To inspire conversations comparing and contrasting life in a different culture;
- To explore what we can learn about the daily routines and environment of another culture through authentic snapshots of daily life;
- To help students establish personal connections to a place and culture they may not have experienced before.

TECH TOOLS INTEGRATED: Google Earth (google.com/earth) and Google Cardboard (vr.google.com/cardboard)

> I've seen first-hand how this activity has the power to alter a student's perception of the world—Google Earth and Cardboard take learning about culture, something that can be so intangible and abstract, from passive photo viewing to a fast-paced adventure through city streets and places you wouldn't find on a postcard. *(Alyssa Marcangelo, Elementary French Teacher)*

In order to inspire young students to make connections between their everyday lives and the Parisian culture, K–2 French Immersion teacher Alyssa Marcangelo uses Google Earth and Google Cardboard to create scavenger hunts to help scaffold these connections.

Alyssa introduces the Google Earth scavenger hunts through a read-aloud of the book *A Walk in Paris* by Salvatore Rubbino. In the book, a grandfather takes his granddaughter on a walk through the City of Light. They stop at famous monuments, patisseries, and markets, and take time to marvel at the city's architectural features and notice other small details unique to Paris. After reading the book as a class, Alyssa's students go on their own "walk in Paris" using Google Earth to complete a scavenger hunt looking for all the places and things mentioned in the story. All students receive their own checklist of items to search for, then each child picks a place in Paris on Google Earth to explore in Street View. They never use the search bar to look for items on the scavenger hunt—they only search in the locations students select.

Figure 8.1 Students in Ms. Marcangelo's class participating in an interactive share-aloud of a virtual tour of Paris on Google Earth.

Alyssa creates scavenger hunts as a way to inspire conversation between her students and their pen pals. Her students correspond with students at their sister school in Paris by using Google Earth. They go on a scavenger hunt around their sister school to see if they can find places that they know about, places they want to learn more about, or simply things that the two schools have in common. Exploring the surrounding area in Street View creates "shared experiences" with her students and their pen pals. They see things that their pen pals see and experience on a daily basis, or find places that they have in common. For example, her students were thrilled to discover that their sister school has a Starbucks across the street, just like they do! This allowed them to start wondering if their pen pals stopped there with their parents on the way to school just like kids in their class do—maybe they even have a favorite drink in common. This activity changed the types of questions her students wanted to ask their pen pals. Questions shifted from things like "What's your favorite color?" to "Have you ever been to this café? The menu looks really delicious!" Google Street View offers incredible opportunities for her students to engage with their pen pals and enhances the relationship they develop throughout the year.

Finding all the items on the list is not the main goal of the assignment. The scavenger hunt is used as a fun way to engage students in conversation and help them apply what they have learned about the French language, history, and culture.

Alyssa brings signage into the activity every time they go on a scavenger hunt to highlight the fact that there are so many shared words between English and French. Additionally, Alyssa teaches her students that a bright-green cross designates pharmacies in Paris, which is important to know if they ever travel to France and need to know where to find medicine or first-aid equipment. This is always done as a whole-group activity because of the nature of the conversation it aims to inspire.

As they complete the scavenger hunt, her students always notice things that aren't on the list:

- Many of the buildings in Paris look the same—everything matches. Even schools blend into the architecture and often aren't stand-alone buildings surrounded by trees and a playground, like her students may be used to.

- Many street signs are familiar, or very similar: traffic lights, crosswalks, no left turn signs, and so on.

- Telephone numbers are written very differently.

- Many people travel by scooter or bike as opposed to by car.

For an even more authentic experience, her students explore locations from the scavenger hunt using expedition-style Google Cardboard to deepen the immersive experience and feel as if they are really standing in the streets of Paris, on the Eiffel Tower, in the Louvre, or at the Palace of Versailles. Cardboard gives them a new perspective to learn about the city of Paris and make it all the more personal.

Figure 8.2 A scavenger hunt list Ms. Marcengalo created for her students to locate items in Google Earth.

Learn More: Detroit Country Day School's Blog, Passport to Adventure: Bringing Paris into the Classroom (goo.gl/3jTiqx)

Table 8.1 addresses how the project incorporates the Triple E Framework components of engagement, enhancement, and extension.

Table 8.1 Case Study 1: Alignment with the Triple E Framework

Engage	Going on a "virtual field trip" and exploring real, new locations immediately pulls students into the lesson and keeps them on task. They are able to make text-to-self connections based on the book they read as well as what they experience in their everyday lives.
	The students co-use the technology with their sister classroom, and co-explore Google Earth together. They make connections and construct knowledge in a way that is time-on-task and authentic.
Enhance	Google Earth provides students with authentic images of daily life in Paris, allowing them to develop a more sophisticated understanding of life in a foreign country.
	Street View and Google Cardboard give students the chance to demonstrate what they have learned about the city of Paris in as close to a "real-life" setting as you can achieve in the classroom. The technology moves the French city and culture from the abstract world to that of real places and experiences.
Extend	The Google Earth and Cardboard technologies allow students to make deep connections between their everyday life experiences and the life of someone living in Paris.
	The technology allows students to have connections with other students across the globe and look for authentic connections between their everyday experiences.
	This activity equips students with tools and life skills one can use when traveling to a foreign country, and helps students build an appreciation and understanding of other cultures.

Case Study 2
PLTW Sun, Moon, and Stars

Program Information

GRADE LEVEL: Grade 1

SUBJECT AREA: Science (Math, Writing, and ELA)

TEACHERS AND LESSON AUTHORS:

- Brooke Stidham, First-Grade Teacher, Ann Arbor STEAM School
- Elizabeth Pierce, First-Grade Teacher, Ann Arbor STEAM School

LOCATION: Ann Arbor, Michigan

ISTE STANDARDS: Empowered Learner, Knowledge Constructor, Creative Communicator, Global Collaborator

LEARNING GOALS/STANDARDS MET:

Next Generation Science Standards (NGSS):

- 1-PS4-2. Make observations to construct an evidence-based account that objects in darkness can be seen only when illuminated.

- 1-ESS1-1. Use observations of the sun, moon, and stars to describe patterns that can be predicted.

- 1-ESS1-2. Make observations at different times of year to relate the amount of daylight to the time of year.

- K-2-ETS1-1. Ask questions, make observations, and gather information about a situation people want to change to define a simple problem that can be solved through the development of a new or improved object or tool.

- K-2-ETS1-2. Develop a simple sketch, drawing, or physical model to illustrate how the shape of an object helps it function as needed to solve a given problem.

- K-2-ETS1-3. Analyze data from tests of two objects designed to solve the same problem to compare the strengths and weaknesses of how each performs.

Common Core State Standards (ELA):

- CCSS.ELA.LITERACY.W.1.2 Write informative/explanatory texts in which they name a topic, supply some facts about the topic, and provide some sense of closure.

- CCSS.ELA.LITERACY.SL.1.1 Participate in collaborative conversations with diverse partners about Grade 1 topics and texts with peers and adults in small and larger groups.

- CCSS.ELA.LITERACY.SL.1.1a Follow agreed-upon rules for discussions (e.g., listening to others with care, speaking one at a time about the topics and texts under discussion).

- CCSS.ELA.LITERACY.SL.1.1b Build on others' talk in conversations by responding to the comments of others through multiple exchanges.

- CCSS.ELA.LITERACY.SL.1.1c Ask questions to clear up any confusion about the topics and texts under discussion.

- CCSS.ELA.LITERACY.SL.1.5 Add drawings or other visual displays to descriptions when appropriate to clarify ideas, thoughts, and feelings.

- CCSS.ELA.LITERACY.RL.1.1 Ask and answer questions about key details in a text.

Common Core State Standards (Math):

- CCSS.MATH.CONTENT.1.MD.A.1. Order three objects by length; compare the lengths of two objects indirectly by using a third object.
- CCSS.MATH.CONTENT.1.MD.A.2. Express the length of an object as a whole number of length units, by laying multiple copies of a shorter object (the length unit) end to end; understand that the length measurement of an object is the number of same-size length units that span it with no gaps or overlaps.

TECHNOLOGY TOOLS INTEGRATED: SkyMap Free (goo.gl/gth8GS), Moon Globe (goo.gl/JJdu1d), still camera, 3D pen, Skype (skype.com), Seesaw (web.seesaw.me), Popplet (popplet.com) and Story Creator (goo.gl/Wge1bc)

> Since we cannot take a trip to the stars or moon, they found it very interesting to explore these places right on their iPad. Although all students have access to 1:1 technology via their iPads, these types of tasks are very cooperative—they are sharing what they see, asking questions, and presenting new knowledge gained to their peers.
> *(Brooke Stidham, First-Grade Teacher and PBL Coordinator)*

The first-grade teaching team at Ann Arbor STEAM was interested in a project that helped students understand the patterns of the sun, moon, and stars in order to connect their learning to everyday life experiences. Utilizing Project Lead the Way curriculum, they developed a unit where first-grade students used their knowledge of the patterns of the sun and UV light to design a structure for their school's playground that would provide protection from the sun. Students participated in a "design thinking" process as part of this unit; everything was documented into their design team's Seesaw Learning Log, where they were able to share their data, reflect up on it, and ultimately design their structure.

The unit began with the driving question, *How can we, as astronomers and engineers, build a structure to protect us from the sun?* Next, the first-grade students interviewed kindergarten students to gather data about what is desired in a playground structure. Following the interviews, the first graders used SkyMap and Moon Globe to understand the patterns of the moon, sun, and stars. They took pictures of the playground throughout the day to document the movement of the sun and shadows in various locations. Students also were able to Skype with a real astronaut and ask him questions about the sun, Earth, and moon. After learning about the sun, moon, and stars and gathering data, the students built a model of their playground structure. The students were asked to design and build a playground structure that would protect the children from the sun. As they were learning about the sun, moon, and stars, students were collecting research on each topic, which was compiled into an informational text. The students organized this research in their Seesaw Learning Log and Popplet. Popplet is a mind-mapping software that allows the students to brainstorm and make connections between their research and observations. Using Popplet as a collaborative team allowed them all to share research and co-construct connections. Students ultimately built their model for the playground, based on authentic images from their playground.

Figure 8.3 Students using the Moon Globe app to explore the surface and shadows. They were very intrigued with the "dark side" of the moon!

During reading and writing time, the students learned about the different elements of informational text (as well as other genres) and how to write an informational text. Students presented their model of the playground in small groups, along with their informational text on the sun, moon, and stars. They also presented their model at a public expo at the school.

Table 8.2 addresses how the project incorporates the Triple E Framework components of engagement, enhancement, and extension.

Table 8.2 Case Study 2: Alignment with the Triple E Framework

Engage	Co-engagement occurred in many ways through the technology tools. Since they cannot take a trip to the stars or moon, the students benefitted from being able to explore faraway places right on their iPad. These types of tasks are very cooperative and collaborative—they are sharing what they see, asking questions, and presenting new knowledge gained to their peers. Seesaw journaling gave students an opportunity to co-construct design ideas and data as well as share with others to receive constructive feedback while probing and reflecting.
Enhance	The space exploration apps allowed the young students to grasp a very difficult concept—space. These apps could help scaffold and give some tangible aspect to the content lectures and nonfiction read-alouds. The 3D pens allowed the students to make their structures in a more realistic three-dimensional form, rather than just using paper and pencil. The pen allowed them to create intricate details on their structures. Integrating Popplet for graphic organizing allowed the students to make their thinking visible using text and data that they had been collecting. It also provided them with opportunities to use higher-order thinking skills and to collaborate, create, reflect, and synthesize information.
Extend	With the SkyMap and Moon Globe apps, many students began noticing different constellations in the night sky and charting the moon phases; they came inside from recess and realized they were feeling warmer due to the sun's UV rays! Without prompting, students navigated the playground differently, noticing shadows and places where there was or wasn't shade while also comparing it to their own backyards. The classes were also able to Skype in experts, such as an astronaut, to share and answer students' questions. This helped them connect with actual scientists doing space-related science. Using cameras to record and view authentic pictures from early morning to late evening allowed students to see the shadow pattern on their playground, so they could design a structure with the best opportunity for shade during recess times.

Learn More: 1st Grade STEAM @ Northside website (goo.gl/GzbXu4)

See Figures 8.4 through 8.9 for more images from the project.

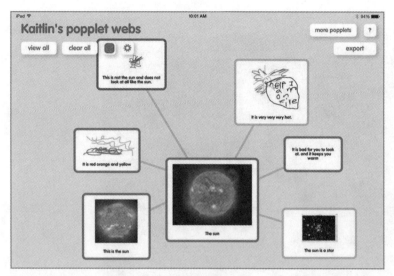

Figure 8.4 Students created Popplets as graphic organizers throughout the unit. This was often a reflection on what they had learned or read. Later, they used these notes to write their final informational book. They also made Popplets during guided reading lessons (either in groups or individually) to make connections between books (text-to-text, text-to-self, and text-to-world—or text-to-project, in this case!).

Figure 8.5 Students Skyped with a real astronaut to ask questions about the relationship between the sun, moon, and earth.

Figure 8.6 Students use a 3D pen to add detail to their play structures.

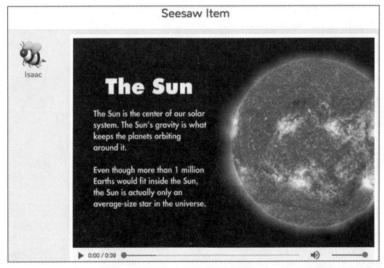

Figure 8.7 Students designed their structure to protect them from the sun on the playground. They documented their learning in Seesaw and created presentations in the tool.

Figure 8.8 The students drew over photographs (using their Seesaw Journal) to show where they wanted their structure and what it should look like (based on a first draft they had drawn on paper).

Figure 8.9 Students evaluated play structure models to see if they protected people from the sun and UV rays.

Case Study 3
Flint Water Crisis: A Project-Based Unit

Program Information

GRADE LEVEL: Grade 3

SUBJECT AREA: Literacy/ELA

TEACHER AND LESSON AUTHOR: Kelly Grahl, Teacher at Cahoon Elementary Magnet School, Tampa, Florida

LOCATION: Lesson was taught at Carpenter Elementary School, Ann Arbor, Michigan

ISTE STANDARDS: Empowered Learner, Digital Citizen, Creative Communicator, Global Collaborator

LEARNING GOALS/STANDARDS MET:

- Students will learn about human rights and how to discuss the purpose of human rights.
- Students will make connections between human rights and our study of the Flint Water Crisis.

Common Core State Standards:

- CCSS.ELA-LITERACY.RI.3.2: Determine the main idea of a text; recount the key details and explain how they support the main idea.
- CCSS.ELA-LITERACY.W.3.2: Write informative/explanatory texts to examine a topic and convey ideas and information clearly.
- CCSS.ELA-LITERACY.W.3.6: With guidance and support from adults, use technology to produce and publish writing (using keyboarding skills) as well as to interact and collaborate with others.
- CCSS.ELA-LITERACY.W.3.10: Write routinely over extended time frames (time for research, reflection, and revision) and shorter time frames (a single sitting or a day or two) for a range of discipline-specific tasks, purposes, and audiences.

TECH TOOLS INTEGRATED: Piktochart (piktochart.com), Google Hangouts, YouTube, and Google Docs

> Part of creating authentic learning experiences for children is
> recognizing the integral part that technology plays in their lives.
> Technological literacy is a 21st century skill that is already required of
> our students in their everyday lives and certainly will be in their lives
> as productive adults. *(Kelly Grahl)*

As events surrounding high lead levels in the water sources of Flint, Michigan,
unfolded during 2015, students in Kelly Grahl's third-grade class at Carpenter
Elementary School in Ann Arbor, Michigan, expressed concern about their friends
and family in Flint, as well as the condition of the drinking water in their own
community. Hearing this, Kelly began to wonder, *How do we show that we care when
a tragedy has happened?* He shared this concern with his students, and together
they brainstormed some answers to this question. Everyone agreed that they could
communicate with students in Flint to show that they care.

Responding to this, guided by Ann Arbor report card standards and Common Core
State Standards for third grade on informational text and writing, Kelly sought
to connect his students with students just like them in Flint. Luckily, he found a
group of wonderful teachers at Durant-Tuuri-Mott Elementary School who agreed
to be their third-grade pen pals. Feature writing and growing informational text
literacy is an essential thread woven throughout the standards for third-grade
learners. Rooted in the interests of his students, and with standards in mind, they
set out to show they care in a different way: *by teaching others about the issue.* Kelly's
class embarked on a three-week research project learning about the importance of
water in their environment, the effects of lead on the body, the connections between
Flint and their own community, what Universal Human Rights are, and discovering the utility of various informational text features.

The unit began with a video ("We Are Born Free"), through which students learned
about and shared their thoughts on universal human rights. They immediately got to
work researching what had happened in Flint and began crafting their first pen-pal
letters. Their research process included flipping the classroom with YouTube videos
about the crisis in Flint, like "Residents of Flint Tell How Their Lives Have Changed"
(goo.gl/p5g9zN), as well as finding reliable resources online to learn more about the
science and human rights issues behind the disaster. Then they began to brainstorm
how and if having lead in the drinking water violated the human rights of the third
graders in Flint.

Eventually, after using both technology and analog forms of communication, the students were able to collaborate on developing a digital informational text with Piktochart about the Flint Water Crisis through the eyes of third graders in Flint. This informational text was shared publicly for others to learn about the water crisis and how it impacts the children of Flint. The books were published in both digital and analog format and put into the school's library for future students to read and learn about the Flint Water Crisis.

Table 8.3 addresses how the project incorporates the Triple E Framework components of engagement, enhancement, and extension.

Table 8.3 Case Study 3: Alignment with the Triple E Framework

Engage	Students were jointly engaged in the learning process (co-use of the digital tools and researching in teams).
	The technology allowed students to focus on the task at hand rather than being distracted from the learning goals.
Enhance	Piktochart allowed students to co-construct and share their knowledge with others. In addition, the online resources helped students get a full picture of the real issues that residents of Flint were experiencing.
	Synchronous digital tools helped connect the third-grade classrooms.
	The tools also allowed for the higher-order thinking skills of creation and synthesis of knowledge, rather than simple consumption of information.
Extend	The technology (YouTube, Google Docs, and Piktochart) in this lesson allowed students to make deep connections between their everyday life experiences and the life of students (their same age) living in a place where there is an environmental crisis.
	This activity equipped students with the technology know-how and life skills useful for building relationships with others, such as investigation, communication, and collaboration.

Learn More: Kelly Grahl Home Page (kellygrahl.com)

See Figures 8.10 through 8.12 for images from the project.

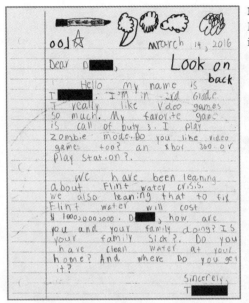

Figure 8.10 A letter from a student in Mr. Grahl's class to a third-grade pen pal in Flint.

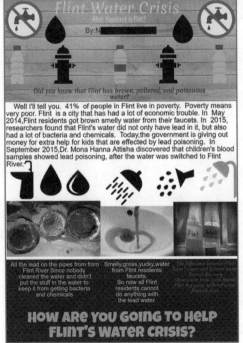

Figure 8.11 A team of students' final informational text (created with Piktochart) that went into the class's collaborative book.

Figure 8.12 Another team from Mr. Grahl's class, sharing their collaborative work about the Flint Water Crisis.

Case Study 4
Elapsed Time and Sled Dog Racing

Program Information

GRADE LEVEL: Grade 4

SUBJECT AREA: Math

TEACHER AND LESSON AUTHOR: Todd Hausman, Fifth-Grade Classroom Teacher, Burlington-Edison School District

LOCATION: Burlington, Washington

ISTE STANDARDS: Empowered Learner, Knowledge Constructor

LEARNING GOALS/STANDARDS MET:

- Washington State Performance Expectation 4.4.C: Estimate and determine elapsed time using a calendar, a digital clock, and an analog clock.

Common Core State Standards:

- CCSS.MATH.CONTENT.4.MD.A.1: Know relative sizes of measurement units within one system of units including: km, m, cm; kg, g; lb., oz.; l, ml; hr, min, sec.

- CCSS.MATH.CONTENT.4.MD.A.2: Use the four operations to solve word problems involving distances, intervals of time, liquid volumes, masses of objects, and money, including problems involving simple fractions or decimals, and problems that require expressing measurements given in a larger unit in terms of a smaller unit.

- CCSS.MATH.CONTENT.4.NF.B.3.D: Solve word problems involving addition and subtraction of fractions referring to the same whole and having like denominators, e.g., by using visual fraction models and equations to represent the problem.

- CCSS.MATH.CONTENT.4.NF.C.7: Compare two decimals to hundredths by reasoning about their size.

TECH TOOLS INTEGRATED: Wikispaces or Kidblog website, Iditarod Live GPS website (iditarod.com/edu)

> Elapsed time is actually a really tricky concept for a lot of students
> and the Iditarod is a great opportunity for them to use real authentic
> data to explore elapsed time. *(Todd Hausman)*

In order to help students connect the tricky mathematical concept of elapsed time, predictions, and real-world experiences, fourth-grade teacher Todd Hausman developed a unit around the Iditarod Trail Sled Dog Race in Alaska. As part of their unit of study, pairs of students selected a musher to follow during the race session. The students learned how to find the mean (average) traveling speed of their chosen Iditarod musher and predict the elapsed time between checkpoints. In order to do this in real time, the students used the Iditarod live GPS website to track the mushers as they moved from checkpoint to checkpoint each day. Prior to starting the project, Mr. Hausmann also set up a class Wikispaces website, which is where the student teams logged in and posted their predictions, reviewed their classmate's predictions, and got feedback from their teacher.

Mr. Hausman began with a whole-group discussion to explain the purpose of the lesson (estimating/predicting/measuring elapsed time). Next he modeled to the class how to navigate the live GPS tracking on the Iditarod website. In addition to modeling the technology, Mr. Hausman also modeled how to estimate and measure elapsed time by asking the class to make a prediction using an Iditarod musher as an example. Together, through guided practice and using the live GPS website, the class estimated how long it would take the musher to get from his or her current checkpoint to the next checkpoint.

The students were then asked to pair up and use laptops to log in to the Iditarod website to view the race standings. They selected a musher to follow and recorded their musher's departure time from the last checkpoint. The students estimated the travel time of their musher to the next checkpoint and predicted their musher's arrival time there. They then posted their predictions on Wikispaces. The following day, the students compared the actual results with their predictions from the previous day. As a final assessment, the students wrote a math equation to justify their prediction.

Table 8.4 addresses how the project incorporates the Triple E Framework components of engagement, enhancement, and extension.

Table 8.4 Case Study 4: Alignment with the Triple E Framework

Engage	Students were jointly engaged in the learning process (co-use of the digital tools). They worked together on the technology. The technology allowed students to focus on the task at hand rather than being distracted from the learning goals. The teacher only had them use the technology after he gave them guided practice of "how to" navigate the live GPS website and the wiki to make their predictions.
Enhance	The live GPS website allowed students to use authentic data to understand their math learning goal. They could also assess how accurate they were in making their predictions as well as check the live tracking 24/7.
Extend	The technology tools (GPS tracking website and Wikispaces) in the lesson allowed students to make deep connections between mathematical use of elapsed time and how it can be used to predict authentic experiences (e.g., live sled dog racing). Many students checked on their musher at home once they learned how to use the live GPS tracker. This technology equipped students with tools and life skills they can utilize when using real data to make inferences and predictions.

Learn More: Teaching Channel (www.teachingchannel.org/videos/technology-and-math)

Case Study 5

UN Poets

Program Information

GRADE LEVEL: Grade 4

SUBJECT AREA: Science, ELA

TEACHER AND LESSON AUTHOR: Evelyn Daugherty, ELA/ESL Teacher, Scarlett Middle School

LOCATION: Lesson was taught at Bach Elementary School in Ann Arbor, Michigan.

ISTE STANDARDS: Empowered Learner, Creative Communicator, Knowledge Constructor and Global Collaborator

LEARNING GOALS/STANDARDS MET:

Common Core State Standards:

- CCSS.ELA-LITERACY.RF.4.4.B: Read grade-level prose and poetry orally with accuracy, appropriate rate, and expression on successive readings.

- CCSS.ELA-LITERACY.RL.4.5: Explain major differences between poems, drama, and prose, and refer to the structural elements of poems (e.g., verse, rhythm, meter) and drama (e.g., casts of characters, settings, descriptions, dialogue, stage directions) when writing or speaking about a text.

TECHNOLOGY TOOLS INTEGRATED: YouTube, iMovie, Google Docs, and UN World Water Day website (www.unwater.org/worldwaterday)

> The students recorded their voices reading the poems, so you can actually click on the links and hear the students read their own poetry reflecting the lessons about how to perform poetry as well as how to write it and, of course, think of expressive language and what we call expensive words and using white space. *(Evelyn Daugherty)*

Evelyn Daugherty was looking for authentic ways teach students how poetry, media, and text can create powerful messages for real audiences. At the time, Evelyn was designing a science unit on water and energy. Ms. Daugherty was aware that throughout history poets have written about water—poets such as Robert Frost and Emily Dickinson. A teaching colleague shared that the United Nations World Water Day website was asking students to put together unique poems about appreciating and conserving water. Consequently, Ms. Daugherty developed a month-long unit to help her fourth-grade students explore how poetry can inspire others to appreciate and conserve water.

The project launched with Ms. Daugherty's students receiving a personalized letter from the United Nations World Water Organization asking the fourth graders to write and share poems in celebration of World Water Day (March 22). The students engaged in a whole-group discussion about what the United Nations is and why it is important to celebrate World Water Day. They were introduced to significant vocabulary from science, and they learned how water is a "natural resource" and how they use large amounts of water in their daily lives. The students then engaged in a cross-curricular unit, where they studied the science behind water and energy and different types of poems and poetic devices.

Figure 8.13 An image of a student's original poem that was turned into an interactive poem with iMovie and posted on the UN website.

Students began discovering how to use performance, language, and structure to create a powerful poem that would inspire others to appreciate and conserve water. During the unit students created seven poems and used Google Docs to collaborate on their poems as they built them. Google Docs allowed students to give feedback to their peers on their work, and with the app's special features, the students learned how to fuse text and art. Using Google Docs, Ms. Daugherty modeled how to give constructive and critical feedback, and she modeled poetry writing and feedback while also monitoring the students' writing via their Google accounts. Because Google Docs allows synchronous editing, Ms. Daugherty could weigh in during the writing process. Throughout the unit, to enhance the experience of reading poetry, students collaborated on the use of different types of media—audio, visual, and text layout. Eventually, the students created original artwork to connect images to the poems and developed an iMovie using these elements to accompany their final poems. In order to understand how to "read" their poetry with expression, students watched videos of students speaking poetry (for an example, see Asha Christensen at goo.gl/yx297Q). Each student recorded himself or herself reading a poem, using oral speaking skills such as intonation, annunciation, and rate of speech. Students learned how to create expression using the audio editing tools in iMovie.

The project culminated in a Poetry Café where students shared poems with parents and members of the community. Finally, with parent permission, students' iMovie poems were shared with the UN World Water Day for official publication on its website.

Table 8.5 addresses how the project incorporates the Triple E Framework components of engagement, enhancement, and extension.

Table 8.5 Case Study 5: Alignment with the Triple E Framework

Engage	Students were jointly engaged in the learning process (co-use of the digital tools). They worked together through the technology.
	The technology tools (YouTube videos, iMovie, Google Docs) allowed students to focus on the task at hand rather than being distracted from the learning goals. The teacher used many instructional strategies, such as guided practice, monitoring, and modeling, to keep them focused on the learning goals when using the technology tools.
Enhance	iMovie allowed students to show their understanding of water as a source of energy through a multi-modal representation, and to share with a global audience.
	Google Docs allowed students to learn how to fuse text and art in order to represent ideas via text. In addition, students and teachers were able to collaborate via Google Docs to give constructive and collaborative feedback.
Extend	The technology in this lesson allowed students to make connections between English language arts, science, and the work of the United Nations around water as an energy source. The publication on the UN website gave the students a global audience.
	This activity equipped students with tools and life skills one can use when communicating to a global audience about an important topic or idea.

Learn More: Fourth Grade Poets (bachpoets.weebly.com/teaching-resources.html)

See Figures 8.14 and 8.15 for more images from the project.

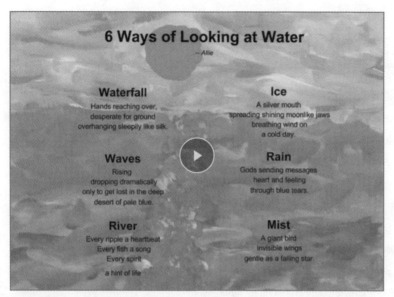

Figure 8.14 An image of a student's original poem that was turned into an interactive poem with iMovie and posted on the UN website.

Figure 8.15 Ms. Daugherty working with students collaborating on poetry that fuses text and image.

Case Study 6
Bridge Challenge Project

Program Information

GRADE LEVEL: Grades 3, 4, and 5

SUBJECT AREA: Science, ELA

TEACHERS AND LESSON AUTHORS:

- Michael Thornton, Classroom Teacher, Agnor-Hurt Elementary
- Julia McGill, Classroom Teacher, Stony Point Elementary
- Mia Shand, Gifted Resource Teacher, Agnor-Hurt Elementary
- Stephanie Passman, Gifted Resource Teacher, Stony Point Elementary
- Gene Osborn, Albemarle County Learning Technology Integrator

LOCATION: Albemarle County Schools, Virginia

ISTE STANDARDS: Empowered Learner, Digital Citizen, Innovative Designer, Creative Communicator, Global Communicator

LEARNING GOALS/STANDARDS MET:

- Students will be able to use their inventory and new tools to create in Minecraft.
- Students will connect with new peers in other places to solve a problem.
- Students will communicate clearly with peers in other places, using technology (Google Hangouts).
- Students will practice being good digital citizens, respectful of digital work of others, and honest in their interactions.

TECH TOOLS INTEGRATED: Minecraft, Google Hangouts

Every single student was 100% engaged. Different components of the challenge were difficult for different students; some did not know how to actually build, some were more timid about communicating with strangers. All students cheered wildly when their teams' bridges were completed. Students found this activity to be important and had agency to solve the problem. *(Stephanie Passman, Stony Point Elementary, Gifted Resource Teacher)*

In order to learn about problem-solving, group management, and communication, the third-, fourth-, and fifth-grade students from two schools in the Albemarle County school district (one urban, one rural) were dropped into a Minecraft world in which they had to work together in teams to build bridges between towers. Each classroom had a team of students on one tower and they had to find a way to build a bridge to reach their partner team on the other tower. Each team was given a set of raw materials to work from in the creative mode of Minecraft and had to figure out how to use those resources to construct a solid structure to connect their tower with the tower of their partner team (in the other classroom).

Figure 8.16 Students in one classroom using Google Hangouts to synchronously connect with their team partners in another classroom and collaborate on their bridge project.

When the teams in one school were stumped, they used Google Hangouts to call their partner team to collaborate and problem-solve. Google Hangouts was open on a computer and projected during the whole experience so that students could come up and communicate with their teammates at the other school. Many students were nervous about using Google Hangouts to contact their partner teams (whom most had never met), but they often overcame their shyness because of wanting to finish their bridge project successfully. The entire project occurred within a Minecraft world. That is where the teams of students first met and built their bridge. Students used Google Hangouts as a platform for talking to teammates. The teams knew they were successful when they were able to connect to their other team and connect their bridge!

Table 8.6 addresses how the project incorporates the Triple E Framework components of engagement, enhancement, and extension.

Table 8.6 Case Study 6: Alignment with the Triple E Framework

Engage	Students were jointly engaged in the learning process (co-use of the digital tools). They worked synchronously on the technology (Google Hangouts and Minecraft).
	The technology allowed students to focus on the task at hand rather than being distracted from the learning goals. The students were able to communicate together in real time as they were problem-solving and building new knowledge.
Enhance	Minecraft allowed teams of students to be logged in simultaneously to the same virtual world, working on the same project, and collaborating on problem-solving skills.
	Minecraft gave the students many options for constructing their bridges, and the students had to collaborate and construct using higher-order thinking skills.
Extend	Google Hangouts gave students in one classroom opportunities to make authentic, real-time connections around problem-solving and building/construction tasks with students in another school who were collaborating on the same project.
	Google Hangouts equipped students with tools and life skills one can use when learning how to communicate with others around a problem-solving task.
	Minecraft allowed the students to operate in a world that was already so important to students and was an authentic environment to them.

See Figure 8.17 for another image from the project.

Figure 8.17 Students working on their bridge project in Minecraft.

Case Study 7
Life Science and Storybooks

Program Information

GRADE LEVEL: Grade 7 and Grade 2

SUBJECT AREA: Science, ELA

TEACHERS AND PROJECT AUTHORS:

- Kyle Dunbar, Technology Integration Specialist
- Michele Meshover, Fourth-Grade Teacher *(taught second grade during this project)*
- Traci Holland, Seventh-Grade Life Science Teacher

LOCATION: Alexandria Public Schools, Alexandria, Virginia

ISTE STANDARDS: Empowered Learner, Digital Citizen, Innovative Designer, Creative Communicator

LEARNING GOALS/STANDARDS MET:

- Students will be able to identify three different types of symbiotic relationships.
- Students will be able to create a story about two animals based on one type of symbiotic relationship.
- Students will be able to use elements of a story to create their story.

Common Core State Standards:

- CCSS.ELA-LITERACY.RST.6-8.7: Integrate quantitative or technical information expressed in words in a text with a version of that information expressed visually (e.g., in a flowchart, diagram, model, graph, or table).
- CCSS.ELA-LITERACY.RST.6-8.4: Determine the meaning of symbols, key terms, and other domain-specific words and phrases as they are used in a specific scientific or technical context relevant to Grades 6–8 texts and topics.
- CCSS.ELA-LITERACY.W.7.4: Produce clear and coherent writing in which the development, organization, and style are appropriate to task, purpose, and audience. (Grade-specific expectations for writing types are defined in standards W.7.1–W.7.3.)
- CCSS.ELA-LITERACY.W.7.6: Use technology, including the internet, to produce and publish writing, and link to and cite sources, as well as to interact and collaborate with others by linking to and citing sources.

TECH TOOLS INTEGRATED: Storykit

> The second graders learned so much—they could identity the type of relationship in every story. And the seventh graders learned so much—how to explain what they know in a compelling, interesting, and memorable way. *(Kyle Dunbar)*

The seventh-grade life science students in Alexandria Public Schools were learning about symbiosis in science class. In order to give the students a more authentic understanding of symbiotic relationships, the seventh-grade classroom teacher, Traci Holland, collaborated with the second-grade teacher, Michele Meshover, and the district technology integration specialist, Kyle Dunbar. They came up with a cross-curricular way for the seventh-grade students to teach the second-grade students about symbiosis through using their language arts skills. Ms. Holland's seventh-grade students worked in pairs to develop stories for second graders about symbiotic relationships. The stories included graphics, text, and audio.

The seventh-grade students used the Storykit app to create their storybook. Storykit allowed the students to create stories using a mixed-media approach with images, audio recordings, photos, drawings, and text. The teachers chose Storykit because it gave students choices for expressing their story, yet, because of its simplicity, it did not distract them with bells and whistles.

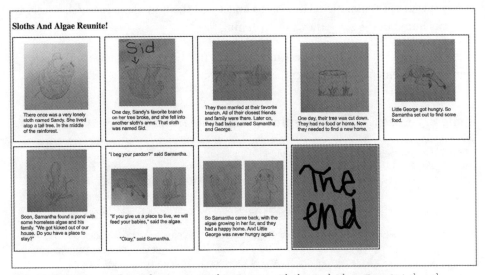

Figure 8.18 A seventh-grade team's symbiosis story, *Sloths and Algae Reunite!,* that they created in Storykit for second graders.

Each seventh-grade team was assigned a different symbiotic relationship (such as mutualism, commensalism, or parasitism) that they had to create a story about for second graders. Before they got started with Storykit, the students worked with their partner to create a story map on paper to use as a guide for creating their project in the app. The teachers created a model of a symbiosis story in Storykit so the seventh graders understood exactly what they were supposed to create. Using the model, the teachers guided the students through the elements of a story and showed them how to identify pieces of the symbiotic relationship in the story. The teachers then used guided practice to help the students understand the steps of creating a story in Storykit, showing them not only how to navigate the tool but also the types of thinking that they should be doing when developing a story (e.g., carefully constructing images that help convey the message in the story). The seventh-grade students used a story graph to develop their story, including literary elements such as plot, setting, and plot twists to demonstrate their understanding of the symbiotic relationship.

Students' final stories were published online and shared in-person with the second graders. When sharing with the second graders, the seventh graders explained the different types of symbiotic relationships and asked them to identify which relationship was found in the story they were listening to.

Table 8.7 addresses how the project incorporates the Triple E Framework components of engagement, enhancement, and extension.

Table 8.7 Case Study 7: Alignment with the Triple E Framework

Engage	Students were jointly engaged in the learning process (co-use of the digital tools). The students loved the chance to co-write a creative story and to use the interactive elements of the Storykit app to do so (the simplicity of Storykit helped them focus on the task at hand). The ability to add sound and digital illustrations made writing this story more exciting and more accessible for many students.
Enhance	The technology in this lesson gave students a chance to show what they know by using higher-order thinking skills of creation and construction in Storykit. Asking them to create a story instead of answering multiple-choice questions really pushed them to apply their learning. Furthermore, trying to explain symbiotic relationships to second graders revealed if they really understood the fundamental characteristics of these relationships.
Extend	Integrating Storykit allowed students to make cross-curricular connections between science and story writing for an authentic audience.

Learn More: Learning with Meaning, Storytime with Storykit (goo.gl/Q9qyp9)

See Figure 8.19 for another image from the project.

Figure 8.19 Seventh-grade students sharing their symbiosis stories with second graders.

Case Study 8
All-American Road Trip

Program Information

GRADE LEVEL: Grade 6

SUBJECT AREA: Math and Social Studies

TEACHER AND LESSON AUTHOR: Tammy Church, Math and Design Technology Teacher, Washtenaw International Middle Academy

LOCATION: Ypsilanti, Michigan

ISTE STANDARDS: Empowered Learner, Knowledge Constructor, Creative Communicator, Innovative Designer, Computational Thinker

LEARNING GOALS/STANDARDS MET:

Common Core State Standards:

- CCSS.MATH.CONTENT.6.RP.A.1: Understand the concept of a ratio and use ratio language to describe a ratio relationship between two quantities.

- CCSS.MATH.CONTENT.6.RP.A.2: Understand the concept of a unit rate a/b associated with a ratio a:b with b ≠ 0, and use rate language in the context of a ratio relationship.

- CCSS.MATH.CONTENT.6.RP.A.3.A: Make tables of equivalent ratios relating quantities with whole-number measurements, find missing values in the tables, and plot the pairs of values on the coordinate plane. Use tables to compare ratios.

- CCSS.MATH.CONTENT.6.RP.A.3.B: Solve unit rate problems including those involving unit pricing and constant speed.

- CCSS.MATH.CONTENT.6.RP.A.3.C: Find a percent of a quantity as a rate per 100 (e.g., 30% of a quantity means 30/100 times the quantity); solve problems involving finding the whole, given a part and the percent.

- CCSS.MATH.CONTENT.6.RP.A.3.D: Use ratio reasoning to convert measurement units; manipulate and transform units appropriately when multiplying or dividing quantities.

National Council for the Social Studies:

- NCSS-C3: D2.Geo.2.6-8. Use maps, satellite images, photographs, and other representations to explain relationships between the locations of places and regions, and changes in their environmental characteristics.

- NCSS-C3: D2.Geo.3.6-8. Use paper based and electronic mapping and graphing techniques to represent and analyze spatial patterns of different environmental and cultural characteristics.

TECHNOLOGY MATERIALS: iPads, Google My Maps

> We want real-world applications in math. We want children to be able to apply math to their lives. *(Tammy Church)*

Sixth-grade math and social studies teacher Tammy Church decided she wanted her students to have a real-world summative assessment of their understanding of proportions, rates, and averages in mathematics, as well as regional geography and mapping skills. Mrs. Church asked her sixth graders to plan a road trip across the United States. As part of their planning, the students had lots of choice but a strict budget and some criteria that they had to adhere to (just like many families who are looking to take a week-long vacation). The students became travel agents and had to plan a week-long road trip for a family of four that began and ended at their school in Ypsilanti, Michigan, and had at least four stops along the way. The road trip was supposed to be a vacation for family fun and entertainment, and costs for the entire trip were limited to $2500. The students created their own itinerary and designed a budget for a mode of transportation, gas, lodging, entertainment, and food. The road trip project was designed to help students apply concepts from both math and geography to a real-world situation. They used Google My Maps to create an interactive map and route for the trip; to search for rental cars, family entertainment spots, and hotels along the way; and to determine costs. Each road trip was unique; students were given the freedom to go anywhere in the United States (as long as they stayed within their budget!). This project has a variety of real-world applications and takes students beyond simply solving math problems on a worksheet or reading a map on paper. Some of the math skills that the students had to use include proportions, averages, mileage, distance, units, ratios, rates, and percentages.

Figure 8.20 Sixth-grade students presenting their final road trip to their peers.

Ultimately, each student created an artifact, which was a trip itinerary and guide for the family to take with them, outlining the travel routes, hours of travel, and restaurant and lodging suggestions that met their budgetary requirements. The trip guide had to include ratio relationships, unit rates (such as unit pricing and constant speed), a graph of rates created from a table or ratios, and calculations of percent. The students were given a choice as to how to present their road trip (digital presentation tools, posters, or traditional papers).

Table 8.8 addresses how the project incorporates the Triple E Framework components of engagement, enhancement, and extension.

Table 8.8 Case Study 8: Alignment with the Triple E Framework

Engage	Students were encouraged to use websites that allowed them to focus on the task at hand (such as Google My Maps or car rental comparison sites) and to use higher-order cognitive thinking skills, such as inquiry and analysis, rather than a "drill and practice" piece of software.
Enhance	The technology in this lesson gave students a chance to use their higher-order thinking skills to investigate and inquire about an authentic road trip, based not only on their own interest but also on a specific budget and time. Using authentic tools via the internet allowed them to have accurate and real-world data to work from.
Extend	The technology in this lesson allowed students to bridge their academic understanding of geography and algebra with authentic experiences that could occur in their lives, such as learning how to measure routes via online mapping tools, calculating gas mileage based on real car rental fees, or comparing car rental rates on various websites.

Learn More: Digital Promise, How One School Hit the Road with Technology (digitalpromise.org/2015/11/25/how-one-school-hit-the-road-with-technology/)

Case Study 9
Graphing Stories

Program Information

GRADE LEVEL: Grade 9

SUBJECT AREA: Math

TEACHER AND PROJECT AUTHOR: Tom Ward, High School Math Teacher, Greenhills School

LOCATION: Ann Arbor, Michigan

ISTE STANDARDS: Knowledge Constructor, Creative Communicator, Innovative Designer, Computational Thinker

LEARNING GOALS/STANDARDS MET:

- Represent and solve equations and inequalities graphically. Linear and exponential; learn as general principle

Common Core State Standards:

- CCSS.MATH.CONTENT.HSS.ID.A.1: Represent data with plots on the real number line (dot plots, histograms, and box plots).

- CCSS.MATH.CONTENT.HSS.MD.B.7: Analyze decisions and strategies using probability concepts (e.g., product testing, medical testing, pulling a hockey goalie at the end of a game).

TECHNOLOGY TOOLS INTEGRATED: Mobile Devices, Vine (or any video capturing app or tool on a mobile device), Graphing Stories (graphingstories.com)

Some of the students wanted to record a group member riding one of those wheelie scooters down a ramp. They wanted to graph the person's height off the ground. But wait! What would that graph look like? Of course, it would be constant if they are referring to height off the floor, but decreasing if they are talking elevation. That conversation happened in my class. That is deep mathematical thought in an Algebra I classroom. *(Tom Ward)*

Ann Arbor Greenhills School math teacher Tom Ward was searching for a way to connect his students' understanding of mathematical graphing to their everyday experiences. After viewing Dan Meyer's graphic stories website, Mr. Ward was inspired to develop a similar project with his own students. Mr. Ward asked his ninth graders to create their own graphing stories using their cell phones, iPads, or iTouches, and the Vine app. Mr. Ward selected Vine because it is popular with the students but also an easy tool for creating short videos. The students were placed in teams of three and asked to brainstorm an everyday experience that they would like to figure out how to graph. First, the students storyboarded the experience, considering and predicting whether or not the data in the graph would be discrete or continuous. The students then went out and filmed their experience using the Vine app on their mobile devices. After capturing the video, the students were able to start and stop the video in order to figure out how to put it into graphical form. Then they shared their graphing stories with the class and discussed the mathematics involved in these everyday experiences.

Table 8.9 addresses how the project incorporates the Triple E Framework components of engagement, enhancement and extension.

Table 8.9 Case Study 9: Alignment with the Triple E Framework

Engage	Students were encouraged to co-engage in this project by working in teams around the technology tool on both the creation of the video in Vine as well as the discussion around the video in order to put the data into graphical form.
Enhance	The technology in this lesson gave students a chance to investigate and inquire about an authentic experience as it relates to math. It added value to their learning because it was used to document the experience and review it, which would be difficult to do without the technology (in particular, the review part). The students were using higher-order thinking skills of problem-solving, data collection, graphing, reflecting, and synthesis.
Extend	The use of Vine in this lesson allowed students to make easy connections between their everyday experiences and mathematical graphing. Students were able to use their own mobile devices to document an everyday experience and then review it in order to put it into graph format.

Learn More: Prime Factors, Graphing Stories and Vine: A Match Made in Heaven (goo.gl/g2aAOC)

See Figures 8.21 and 8.22 for images from the project.

Figure 8.21 A student learning how activities in a video game can take on graphical form.

Figure 8.22 Students filming their graphing story.

Case Study 10
Civilization Creation

Program Information

GRADE LEVEL: Grade 9

SUBJECT AREA: Social Studies

TEACHERS AND PROJECT AUTHORS:

- Adam Hellebuyck, Social Studies Teacher, University Liggett School

- Brad Homuth, Social Studies Teacher, University Liggett School

- Scott Pangrazzi, Social Studies Teacher, University Liggett School

LOCATION: Grosse Pointe Woods, Michigan

ISTE STANDARDS: Empowered Learner, Knowledge Constructor, Creative Communicator, Innovative Designer, Computational Thinker, Global Collaborator

LEARNING GOALS/STANDARDS MET:

Historical Thinking Standards in Alignment to Common Core Standards (www.nchs.ucla.edu/history-standards/common-core-standards-1-1)

- **Identify issues and problems in the past** and analyze the interests, values, perspectives, and points of view of those involved in the situation: Students do this through first-hand experiences as a shaper and resident in their digital civilizations.

- **Evaluate alternative courses of action,** keeping in mind the information available at the time, in terms of ethical considerations, the interests of those affected by the decision, and the long- and short-term consequences of each.

- **Formulate a position or course of action** on an issue by identifying the nature of the problem, analyzing the underlying factors contributing to the problem, and choosing a plausible solution from a choice of carefully evaluated options.

- **Evaluate the implementation of a decision** by analyzing the interests it served; estimating the position, power, and priority of each player involved; assessing the ethical dimensions of the decision; and evaluating its costs and benefits from a variety of perspectives.

- **Consider multiple perspectives** of various peoples in the past by demonstrating their differing motives, beliefs, interests, hopes, and fears. Draw comparisons across eras and regions in order to define enduring issues as well as large-scale or long-term developments that transcend regional and temporal boundaries.

TECHNOLOGY MATERIALS: Minecraft

> In this simulation, students spend as much time reflecting upon their work as they spend interacting and creating within Minecraft. Students often have to justify their decisions in daily journal responses, making references to ideas from world history that inspired their work, as well as evaluating how effective their decisions were and how they would improve if they could do this again. *(Adam Hellebuyck)*

A few years ago, in Adam Hellebuyck's world history class, several students used the video game Minecraft to virtually craft monuments to world history for their final exam. The benefits of such a medium were immediately evident: students could build structures and interact in a shared virtual world with none of the material limitations present in real life. Minecraft was also easy to play and a significant portion of the University Liggett School student body was familiar with it. Thus, Mr. Hellebuyck and his colleagues began to employ Minecraft as an integral piece of the course, using it to help teach students about civilizations, civics, geography, and perspectives throughout history.

Incorporating Minecraft into the ninth-grade world history civilizations project engaged students in a more in-depth conceptual understanding of social studies and its impact on everyday life. Students created fictitious civilizations in a virtual world they were free to manipulate, relying upon their understanding of large themes and trends that they learned in their world history course. Since all students populated the same server, they could interact and work together to build complex societies that, with guidance from the course instructors, were able to change and adapt to new situations over time. Changing the simulation to include Minecraft revolution-ized the students' work. Not only did it allow for more natural interactions between civilizations, students could work together much more easily through the game they had than using the paper-and-pencil methods of the original simulation, so Minecraft also altered the way students considered world history.

First, there was the actual "playing" of Minecraft after studying a Big Era in World History. When the students "played" in class or as homework, there was always a clear building assignment for them to complete related to the concepts they were studying. For example, in Big Era 3, while studying the development of the first civilizations, students were tasked with locating a "perfect" location for a city in the game, considering geography and other factors affecting humans in that time. Next, they needed to build a prototype city in that place, including all of the elements common in early cities, which the students had previously studied in class. Finally, the students reflected upon their "play" in the game through a variety of writing assignments, asking them to connect their work in the game to the large themes of world history explored in the class.

The design of the Minecraft civilization project occurred throughout the entire year-long course. The students "played" in Minecraft in corroboration of their other classroom learning experiences. They began working in teams in the "creative" mode of Minecraft and were all given the ability to create their own civilization. This meant finding an environment that they thought would be the best option to settle, build, and sustain life, such as a desert, a wetland, an island, or a high mountain terrain. In addition to building a civilization to sustain life, they also needed to create other facets of civilization, such as a code of laws and other norms in the culture. For example, students decided on forms of government, the organization of society (e.g., matriarchy versus patriarchy), access to education, public resources versus private, taxes, and economic systems. The students reflected upon their learning and decision-making frequently in a Minecraft journal they kept over the course of the project. In this journal, they justified the decisions they made in their virtual civilizations, relying upon evidence from world history. In addition to pre-planned building and interactive activities in the game, the teachers would occasionally create a natural or man-made disaster, such as a dam breaking or a fire, that the students would have to address through their civilizations. The following section highlights how the activities in Minecraft added value to learning goals throughout the course-length project.

Identify issues and problems in the past. In Minecraft, the students often faced similar challenges to those of people in history, and had to problem-solve using the tools and philosophies available at the time. For example, students living in a desert biome immediately discovered how important it was to locate constant sources of water for irrigation and domestic animals; this search for water determined where they would settle, as it did in early river valley civilizations. Through their in-class and in-game studies, they were able to make these comparisons in depth.

Evaluate alternative courses of action. As students all resided within the same world (on the same server) and built civilizations together, there were always many different ways to accomplish the same task. For example, when the students decided they needed a form of government to streamline the decision-making process, many students defaulted to a democratic style of government. However, many other students questioned the value of democracy in an early agrarian society, and the class held a reasoned and informed debate on the merits and pitfalls of democracy, using their study of world history as evidence.

Formulate a position or course of action on an issue. While students were basing their work on their knowledge of historical societies, they were ultimately building their own civilizations and could not always look to history to find the exact solution to a problem that arose. As a result, their work in Minecraft encouraged them to make historical inferences using their knowledge of how various societies addressed similar problems. For example, one teacher-crafted event in the game involved a fictitious migration of nomads into their agricultural territories. The students were asked to write responses addressing how their society would interact with those nomads. Many students based their responses on the various interactions that settled peoples had with the Mongols: some students chose to fight, some chose to offer tribute, and some chose to try to assimilate the nomads into their cultures. All of the responses used evidence from world history to support their ideas.

Evaluate the implementation of a decision. In this simulation, students spent as much time reflecting upon their work outside of the game as they spent interacting and creating within Minecraft. Students often had to justify their decisions in daily journal responses, making references to ideas from world history that inspired their work, as well as evaluating how effective their decisions were and how they would improve if they could do this again.

Consider multiple perspectives. Since the students drew upon many different cultures in world history as inspiration for their creations, they were constantly evaluating the responses of different civilizations across time and space to similar historical issues. Since the students also worked together to build these civilizations, they had to discuss their analyses of various civilizations with their peers, often compromising and merging ideas to solve historical problems.

Table 8.10 addresses how the project incorporates the Triple E Framework components of engagement, enhancement, and extension.

Table 8.10 Case Study 10: Alignment with the Triple E Framework

Engage	Students were encouraged to co-engage with Minecraft. They worked in teams to co-create their societies, compelling them to work together on design and to reflect upon their choices in their civilizations.
	In their Minecraft journals and other writing assignments, students spent as much time reflecting on their work as they spent interacting and creating within Minecraft. Students often had to justify their decisions in daily Minecraft journal responses, making references to ideas from world history that inspired their work, as well as evaluating how effective their decisions were and how they would improve if they could do this again. This kept students on task!
Enhance	Minecraft allowed students choices and the ability to compare and contrast their choices, because the students all resided within the same world (on the same server) and built civilizations together; there were always many different ways to accomplish the same task.
	Minecraft also provided the instructor an opportunity to "intervene" in the worlds and create "man-made" or "natural" disasters such as invasions or floods. This allowed the students to see the real effects of these disasters and to consider how to address them in their societies. Thus, students were using their higher-order thinking skills to apply their understanding of world history to the project, create new civilizations with innovative ideas, analyze their work, and solve problems.
Extend	In Minecraft, the students often faced similar challenges to those of people in history, and had to solve problems using the tools and philosophies available at the time. Students could connect their own everyday experiences in society with choices they were making in Minecraft (forms of payment, water sources, government systems, rules of law, and so on).

Learn More:

- Minecraft: Education Edition Site (education.minecraft.net)
- World History for Us All (Information on the "Big Eras" Approach) (worldhistoryforusall.sdsu.edu)

See Figures 8.23 through 8.25 for images from the project.

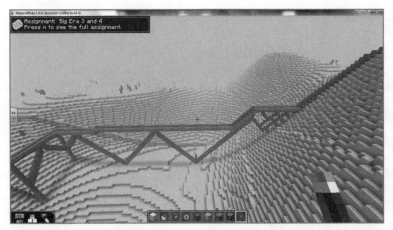

Figure 8.23 Students created an aqueduct to solve irrigation concerns in the civilization.

Figure 8.24 Students created a code of law in their Minecraft civilization.

Figure 8.25 Students set up irrigation systems for their Minecraft civilization.

Case Study 11
E-Mentors

Program Information

GRADE LEVEL: Grade 11

SUBJECT AREA: ELA

TEACHER AND LESSON AUTHOR: Rory Hughes, English Teacher, Redford Thurston High School

LOCATION: Redford, Michigan

ISTE STANDARDS: Empowered Learner, Digital Citizen, Creative Communicator, Global Collaborator

LEARNING GOALS/STANDARDS MET:

Common Core State Standards:

- CCSS.ELA-LITERACY.W.11-12.1: Write arguments to support claims in an analysis of substantive topics or texts, using valid reasoning and relevant and sufficient evidence.

- CCSS.ELA-LITERACY.W.11-12.6: Use technology, including the internet, to produce, publish, and update individual or shared writing products in response to ongoing feedback, including new arguments or information.

- CCSS.ELA-LITERACY.W.11-12.10: Write routinely over extended time frames (time for research, reflection, and revision) and shorter time frames (a single sitting or a day or two) for a range of tasks, purposes, and audiences.

TECHNOLOGY TOOLS: Gmail, Google Forms

One of the most disturbing realities is the lack of positive adult influences in the lives of my students. I don't mean they are all victims of poor parenting. In fact I've found many of the parents to be very supportive. But many of these kids simply do not have the knowledge or the resources to see beyond high school. For many of them, high school graduation is the pinnacle, because maybe they'll be the first in their family to graduate, or they don't know anyone who has ever gone to college. While the research is undeniable about cultural capital and, specifically, connections to real role models, integrating this into a traditional classroom setting is a challenge. *(Rory Hughes)*

Rory Hughes teaches English Language Arts in a high-poverty high school in suburban Detroit, Michigan. He knows that many of his students have dreams of a higher education and professional careers but lack exposure to professionals in their desired careers who can provide some perspective and guidance. Thus, he decided to combine writing with mentorship within the context of a culminating "Five-Year Plan" project, placed after the state test in the Spring. He paired up his students, based on their future goals, with a mentor (some local to Michigan, others far away). As part of the "Five-Year Plan," students produced an E-Portfolio that included exemplar work, a resume, and a personal statement. They then initiated, via email, a conversation with a professional in their field of interest. While many students are proficient with social media and other online tools, few have been explicitly taught how to send an effective email (in fact, many don't even have an email address). This project began several years ago as a blogging assignment but evolved into traditional email because students were showing such a lack of proficiency with email skills and etiquette, which of course are necessary for communicating in college and the workplace.

Here are the steps in the process:

1. The students set up a professional sounding Gmail account.

2. The teacher sends out two Google Forms—one to students and one to people in his/her professional network.

3. The teacher matches the students to the professional according to interest and career path.

4. The students are provided a template from which to craft a professional email to begin the conversation with their mentor. The template includes formatting rules, suggested topics to cover, and questions to ask the mentor.

5. Students pair up for peer revision.

6. After the teacher has reviewed the email and provided feedback, the student sends an email to the mentor, cc'ing the teacher.

7. Once the mentor responds, the teacher helps the student craft an email to keep the conversation going.

8. Students save this email as part of their "Five-Year Plan" assignment.

9. Ideally, correspondence continues throughout high school and beyond.

For more information, see the following examples from the project:

- Google Form to identify career interests (goo.gl/jo2Mip)
- Google Form to potential mentors (goo.gl/ZUue4n)
- Hunter and Pam (attorney) correspondence (goo.gl/uzxoJZ)
- Kaiya and Ben (forensic anthropologist) correspondence (goo.gl/qizCFn)

Table 8.11 addresses how the project incorporates the Triple E Framework components of engagement, enhancement, and extension.

Table 8.11 Case Study 11: Alignment with the Triple E Framework

Engage	The students were able to co-engage through technology. The students knew they were writing for a specific audience, thus the tool allowed them to co-construct dialogue that was appropriate to the audience and to stay on task. Email is a much safer medium for students to be honest, whereas if they were to be introduced to their mentors in person, the communication would have been less thoughtful and less productive.
Enhance	Emailing with experts gave students the opportunity to have another set of "eyes" on their writing. This authentic assessment forced students to be much more reflective in terms of content and mechanics, thus producing significantly better products.
Extend	Email allowed the students to collaborate and connect with actual experts in professional communities. Using the technology, students were able to understand a world beyond their own classroom and see how digital writing has the power to connect them to networks of experts.

Case Study 12
Simulated Gaming

Program Information

GRADE LEVEL: Grades 6–12

SUBJECT AREA: ELA and Social Studies

TEACHERS AND PROJECT AUTHORS:

- Jeff Stanzler, Professor, University of Michigan-Ann Arbor, School of Education
- Jeff Kupperman, Professor, University of Michigan-Flint, School of Education
- K–12 Classroom Teachers across the U.S.

LOCATION: All across the world!

ISTE STANDARDS: Empowered Learner, Digital Citizen, Knowledge Constructor, Creative Communicator, Global Collaborator

LEARNING GOALS/STANDARDS MET:

Common Core State Standards:

- CCSS.ELA-LITERACY.W.11-12.1: Write arguments to support claims in an analysis of substantive topics or texts, using valid reasoning and relevant and sufficient evidence.

- CCSS.ELA-LITERACY.W.11-12.6: Use technology, including the internet, to produce, publish, and update individual or shared writing products in response to ongoing feedback, including new arguments or information.

- CCSS.ELA-LITERACY.W.11-12.10: Write routinely over extended time frames (time for research, reflection, and revision) and shorter time frames (a single sitting or a day or two) for a range of tasks, purposes, and audiences.

TECHNOLOGY TOOLS INTEGRATED:

- Michigan Student Caucus (ICS) (ics.soe.umich.edu/main/section/1)

- Arab-Israeli Conflict (ICS) (ics.soe.umich.edu/main/section/2)

- International Poetry Guild (ICS) (ics.soe.umich.edu/main/section/4)

- Place Out of Time (ICS) (ics.soe.umich.edu/main/section/5)

- Earth Odysseys (ICS) (ics.soe.umich.edu/main/section/3)

We have a trans-historical simulation called, "Place Out of Time," in which university, high school and middle school students come together to discuss an issue by assuming the identities of historical figures. Recently, we did a scenario on the ban in French schools of "conspicuous religious clothing"—head scarves, burqas, things like that—enacted about 10 years ago. Students discuss the issue as if they actually are Napoleon, Barack Obama, or Atticus Finch, so they have to really get inside the heads of these figures. It leverages the ways we think about various professions, in a creative environment.
(Jeff Stanzler)

In the early 1980s, University of Michigan Education Professors Fred Goodman and Edgar Taylor developed the idea of online collaborative projects that created meaningful interactions between K–12 schools and university mentors. Thus the Interactive Communication Simulations (ICS) were born at the University of Michigan School of Education. University Professors Jeff Stanzler and Jeff

Kupperman co-coordinate the program with dozens of middle- and high-school classroom teachers each year. Each project involves meaningful, often intensive, communication among high school students, mentors, and facilitators through interactive, password-protected websites. The simulations are set up so that there are opportunities for personal engagement through character-play, self-expression, and social activism and for the course-based involvement of university-level mentors under the supervision of the project directors.

ICS activities use custom-built environments specific to each project's goals. In addition, secondary teachers can work with the university professors to customize the project for their classroom learning needs. Each year there are five projects that run in the Fall (September–December) and/or Winter (January–April) terms. The projects include the following (descriptions adapted with permission from ics.soe. umich.edu):

Michigan Student Caucus. In the Michigan Student Caucus (MSC), students across the state work online, using a variety of custom-built deliberation, collaboration, and decision-making tools, to create a political platform representing the interests of students across Michigan. The MSC is formally aligned with the Michigan House of Representatives Special Commission on Civic Engagement, and MSC members meet twice a year in Lansing to present formal testimony before House Commission members.

Arab-Israeli Conflict. The Arab-Israeli Conflict Simulation (AIC) is a political and diplomatic character-playing exercise. Its purpose is to immerse participants in the dynamics of national and international politics—and thereby help them to become aware of the complex nature of political reality. AIC enables participants to experience actively, rather than observe passively, complex political activity. The composition of the AIC encompasses 23-character teams, representing the key states and political organizations directly involved in the conflict and outside stakeholders like the United States and other UN Security Council permanent members. Each participating school is assigned several teams across several concurrent simulations. A staff of trained university mentors, under the supervision of project faculty, provides frequent updates, writing support, and guidance to the teams.

International Poetry Guild. The International Poetry Guild (IPG) is a web-based language-arts program that develops students' writing abilities while encouraging them to become critical, appreciative readers of poetry. IPG combines the individualized activity of writing poetry with the teamwork needed to compile "journals" of student work. Through web-based interactions, students exchange their work and ideas with fellow writers around the world. Their poems are also read by a group of University of Michigan student mentors who support and critique participants' work and engage them in an ongoing discussion of poetics and the creative process.

Place Out of Time. Place Out of Time is a simulation of a trial, in which students play guests who come from a range of places and times throughout history to discuss some of the great issues of humankind. The trial takes place (virtually) at the Alhambra Palace in Granada, Spain. Place Out of Time is a writing intensive project for middle and high school students, meant to draw upon their sense of play and the hook of having an audience for their ideas to engage them in thinking differently about the study of history. Student participants and university mentors debate issues and perspectives in character, and move from reading and studying about their characters to a series of opportunities for original research—both historical and creative—as they decide what their character would say about issues that unfolded in places far distant (in time and geography) from their lives.

Earth Odysseys. Earth Odysseys is an interdisciplinary adventure learning activity that "sends" students to places they may never visit in person. Middle school and high school students engage in an intensive interaction with peers from around the world, supported by a staff of university mentors. Student participants learn about the world's geographical and human diversity as well as the rich and varied cultural expressions of its people. In Fall 2016, the Odyssey explored Morocco as seen through the eyes of Fulbright Scholar and high school teacher Nadia Selim.

Table 8.12 addresses how the project incorporates the Triple E Framework components of engagement, enhancement, and extension.

Learn More: Interactive Communications & Simulations at the University of Michigan-Flint and Ann Arbor (ics.soe.umich.edu)

See Figures 8.26 through 8.28 for images from the projects.

Table 8.12 Case Study 12: Alignment with the Triple E Framework

Engage	The students are able to co-engage through technology. The students are collaborating and co-constructing knowledge with other students and mentors through the interactive tools. The tool helps them stay on task because they are fully immersed in the process (not the product) of learning social studies or writing techniques.
Enhance	Learning possibilities are enhanced through the interplay among a variety of elements. Students are connected to an engaged audience of peers; they perform meaningful tasks characterized by a playful spirit, which leverages their creativity and imagination; and they develop rich, ongoing relationships with mentors.
Extend	These highly interactive simulations make manifest the ways in which diplomats, historians, creative writers, and actors see the world and make meaning from it. They extend learning by offering students authentic opportunities to experience how professionals think, how they connect ideas, and how they communicate with real-world audiences.

Figure 8.26 Sample proposal from the Michigan Student Caucus.

Figure 8.27 Place Out of Time courtroom login.

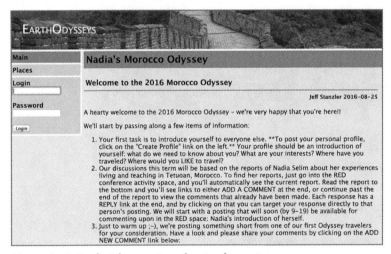

Figure 8.28 Earth Odysseys Introduction for 2016.

Chapter Take-Aways

This chapter shared authentic projects created by K–12 teachers that meet all three areas of the Triple E Framework as well as the 2016 ISTE Standards for Students.

Each case study included the following:

- Information on each program from the teachers who designed and taught the lessons

- Detailed descriptions of each project

- Examples of images from the project and/or tools used in creating the project

- A table outlining how the lesson meet the Triple E Framework

Chapter 9

Instructional Support Strategies

IN ORDER TO SELECT effective applications for classroom learning, teachers need to rely on the effective instructional practices of each content area and look for those practices to be built into the tools. For example, in writing instruction, students need to focus more on the process of learning to write (brainstorming, revision, and editing) and less on the bells and whistles of the final product. Hence, selecting a tool that emphasizes the writing process—in particular, co-engagement around learning to write—is better than selecting a tool that emphasizes a pretty product at the end while students work in isolation.

Even when tools have some effective built-in learning strategies, teachers still need to provide instructional supports for engaging students in the learning goals around the tool. Many of these instructional strategies can come from effective practices in literacy, science, math, and social studies learning. Just as I have never heard of a child that learned to read simply by having a book in their hands, it is rare for software alone to create learning gains without other instructional supports.

> Students are most successful when they are taught how to learn as well as what to learn. *(Brigid Barron and Linda Darling Hammond, 2008)*

Instructional Strategies

Here are some instructional strategies, modified from content-area experts' research (NCSS, 2016; National Council of Science, 2007; Anthony & Walshaw, 2009; Duke and Pearson, 2002), that could be used to help facilitate learning through and with technology tools.

Selecting a "Just Right" Tool

Similar to practices in literacy learning, where we ask students to select a "just right" text or book that meets their Zone of Proximal Development (where they are challenged but not too much), technology should also be adaptable. Teachers should select technology tools that allow their students to meet their learning goals with some scaffolds from the teacher or tool, but it should not be overly challenging or distracting from the learning goals.

Here are some elements to consider for a "just right" tool.

Differentiation. An important part of the "just right" tool is looking for technology that allows for differentiation of learning. Some tools, such as Tween Tribune, allow teachers to select learning levels for different students. This is helpful because students can still participate in the same text, but in a more or less challenging way.

Focus on Learning Task. A "just right" tool will allow the students to easily focus on the learning goals and not be distracted by other features of the device.

Choice. Choice may mean having many options for the students to pursue different interests through the tool. One example may be using software such as Storyboard That to create a comic. While the students are expected to create a comic, there are many different types of characters, settings, objects, and frames to choose from, so they can make it personal or relevant to their everyday experiences. However, choice could also mean allowing students to select from different software tools so they can select the "just right" tool to meet their learning goals.

Modeling

In all content areas, modeling is key to helping students learn to navigate resources. Consequently, modeling how to use technology is key to creating truly engaged learners with technology tools. Modeling should usually occur prior to the students getting the technology tools. Teachers can use direct instruction (in large or small groups) to guide students through the navigation of both the software and the "thinking" that should be occurring as students are using the software. For example, a teacher demonstrating the tool may say, "This is how I search for images on the tool. I need to use keywords to find these images. I want to make sure my keywords describe the images that I am searching for. The type of images that I search for need to reflect the text that I am going to add. I want to make sure my message is clear to my audience, so the image I choose is very important to this message. Would I choose an image of a car when I am talking about an animal in my text? No, I would want to find an image of the animal."

Here are some examples of modeling strategies that work well for technology integration.

Guided Practice and a Gradual Release of Responsibility. Using an "I do, we do, you do" approach to modeling can be effective for students to first see the teacher modeling through direct instruction (no devices in the students' hands). Then the children get their devices (after some instruction on how to treat the devices) and do the learning activity together with the teacher through guided practice. Finally, the teacher releases responsibility to the students so they can try the technology on their own or with others in the class.

Software Tour. This is similar to a "book or chapter tour" in which teachers and students look through the text together. During a software tour, teachers can take their students on a "tour" of the software, asking them to share what they notice about the tool, such as the options for visual representations, and how they might visualize using the tool.

Teacher Think-Aloud. This is a literacy routine for modeling that can be helpful when showing students how to think when navigating software. While demonstrating the software, the teacher will literally talk out loud about what he/she is doing and why he/she is making certain choices in the software.

Co-Use and Co-Engagement

Teachers create structures around the technology tool to allow students to talk about their thinking. This is especially important in tools that do not have collaboration built into them. The ability to co-engage around the tool creates opportunities for students to use higher-order talk such as questioning, reflection, problem-solving, and co-construction of knowledge.

Here are some strategies used in content-area instruction that allow students to talk about text with others.

Turn and Talk. Ask students to stop using their devices and turn and talk to their neighbor about what they are learning, how they are learning it, and what they would like to learn next.

Think, Pair, Share. Similar to turn and talks, ask students to reflect on a specific aspect of the learning, then share with a partner, and eventually share out to the class what they talked about with their partners.

Purposeful Partnering. Asking students to work together on the device, rather than alone, is one way to help them co-construct knowledge and stay on task. Give each partner a purpose and role. For example, the teacher can ask one partner to be the typist, while the other may come up with the content for searches. Or the teacher can ask them to stop and answer a checklist of questions periodically about what they are doing and why.

Switcheroo. This is a fun activity, but also creates co-engagement. Ask students to do a "switcheroo," meaning they stop their work on their device and switch the actual device with another student. They then look over the work of that student, provide feedback (it could be via the software or in person). Sometimes you could even have students build or add to the content—such as creating a collaborative story.

Reflective Thinking Practices

All content areas encourage self and group reflection on learning activities. Using technology is no different. We want to encourage students to reflect on their activities in the software.

Here are some techniques to consider when students are using software that does not encourage active reflective practices.

Self-Reflection. Teach students to use self-reflective strategies as they work on their device (often a teacher can model this with guided practice routines). Students should be asking themselves questions as they engage in the content, such as "I wonder…" or "I notice…." Teaching students to use Visible Thinking strategies can help them learn to ask reflective questions, such as "I see...," "I think...," or "I wonder...." Part of reflecting is also learning how to generate predictions, so the students will want to probe the content in the software more deeply.

Read-Alouds and Interactive Share-Alouds. In effective literacy and math instruction, students are often encouraged to participate in group, reading out loud while the teacher probes with inquiry and questioning strategies. When using technology, students could participate in a similar activity by building or co-constructing ideas in a collaborative piece of software (such as creating a mindmap with Popplet). As they are building, the teacher can ask questions about their learning and students can share out to the class their reflections.

Visual Representations. Teachers can ask students to use technology tools to create visual representations that demonstrate their understanding of the content learning through the software. These representations may be in the form of a graphic organizer, concept map, drawing, movie, animation, digital poster, or even through traditional paper-and-pencil tools.

Elicit Prior Knowledge. Students often learn by connecting what they currently know with new knowledge and ideas. Teachers can integrate strategies around digital tools to help students make these authentic connections. Teachers can use strategies to integrate both students' prior technical skills as well as their content knowledge when selecting tools and designing lessons.

Tech-to-Self Connections. Similar to literacy practices that ask students to make connections between what they are reading and themselves, students should learn to make connections between what they are doing with technology tools and their everyday experiences. Select technology tools that allow students to connect their everyday experiences to the content learning. Also, allow students to select tools to complete an assignment goal, rather than the teacher always selecting for them.

Monitoring Learning

Avoid assuming that a technology tool is accurately monitoring learning because it is collecting data as the student works on the tool.

Here are some tips to help ensure that you are periodically monitoring learning.

Sit Down with Students. Sit down with students as they work on their devices. Ask them informal assessment questions and probe their thinking to see if they are taking up the content knowledge through the device or if you need to redirect them.

Self-monitoring. Teach students how to self-monitor their learning, and assess their ability to do this with technology tools. For example, teach them how to do self-reflective questioning while learning. Give students a checklist with questions they should periodically stop and answer. If they cannot answer them, they can ask the teacher for support, or re-do the activities that they did not understand.

Authentic Context

Create a real-world purpose for the technology use. Teachers can create a context around the assignment so that there is an authentic purpose for using the technology tools. For example, use technology to problem-solve a real-world issue, network with local community members, or advocate for an important cause.

Adding Value and Integrating Strategy

Table 9.1 includes some examples of effective instructional practices from the four major content areas: literacy, social studies, science, and mathematics. The table lists how these strategies can be modified when integrating technology tools and also meet one or more of the Triple E Framework components.

Table 9.1 Tools to Add Value and Integrate Strategy

Technology Integration Strategies	Literacy Learning Strategies	Math Learning Strategies	Social Studies Learning Strategies	Science Learning Strategies	Triple E Level Emphasized Most
Modeling of the tool Guided practice for both navigation and thinking with the tool "I do, we do, you do" approach Software tour	Guided practice Modeling Gradual release of responsibility Chapter tour	Modeling strategies	As new information or skills are presented, teachers facilitate discourse and understanding.	Teachers need to help manage the inquiry process, making sense of data, discussion, and reflection on the results. Instruction should be built incrementally toward more sophisticated understanding and practices.	Engage
Identify the learning goals (reason why you are using the device) Teacher think-aloud, sharing how they are thinking as you navigate a device	Identify purpose of task of reading or writing with explicit instructions and modeling Teacher think-aloud	Selecting tools to support and add value to shared student thinking and knowledge building		Building in time for meta-reflection, where students assess their own degree of understanding and the purpose of the activity	Engage

Continued

Technology Integration Strategies	Literacy Learning Strategies	Math Learning Strategies	Social Studies Learning Strategies	Science Learning Strategies	Triple E Level Emphasized Most
Student share-aloud Turn and talk Purposeful partnering Co-use of tool Switcheroo Active process of hands-on learning with the technology tools	Student think-aloud where children share out loud how they are thinking and what they are doing as they read Children model collaboratively Turn and talk Co-reading	Active participation in large and small group discussions Developing mathematical argumentation through discussion and collaboration	Students discuss values, engage in real-world problem solving, and make reasoned decisions.	Sharing ideas with peers Collaborative classroom discourse that promotes sense-making with higher-order thinking questions is key to supporting learning in science.	Engage
Monitoring and assessing learning as it is happening with the technology tools Teacher sits down with students as they work. Self-monitoring	Monitoring comprehension and periodic assessments Self-questioning	Monitoring mathematical understanding		Ongoing assessment is an integral part of instruction that can foster student learning when appropriately designed and used regularly.	Engage & Enhance

Continued

Technology Integration Strategies	Literacy Learning Strategies	Math Learning Strategies	Social Studies Learning Strategies	Science Learning Strategies	Triple E Level Emphasized Most
Children use inquiry as part of their learning through and with a device. Switcheroo Reflective thinking strategies Visual representations	Reflecting, questioning, re-telling, re-reading, and predicting during reading Visual representations of text (e.g., graphic organizers and mind maps) Talk about the text Student-developed questioning around text	Inquiry learning	Inquiry learning through questions that stimulate decision making, problem solving, and issue analysis	Actively engaging students in thinking scientifically with such practices like inquiry, hypothesizing, and reasoning based on evidence	Enhance
Selecting "just right" technology tools that provide opportunities to differentiate or personalize learning to student's learning levels, interests, and cultural norms Elicit prior knowledge.	Selecting text that is culturally relevant to the student Selecting "just right" or well-suited texts for students, reading level and interest level	Building mathematical understanding based on students' interests, previous knowledge, and experiences	Design learning to leverage students' prior skills and make meaningful connections and expand their knowledge and viewpoints.	Prior student knowledge and questions should be linked to experiences with experiments, data.	Enhance & Extend

Continued

Technology Integration Strategies	Literacy Learning Strategies	Math Learning Strategies	Social Studies Learning Strategies	Science Learning Strategies	Triple E Level Emphasized Most
Selecting technology devices that leverage connections between student learning and student everyday life experiences Tech-to-self connections Creating an authentic context	Expanding understanding of text for present-day learners Text-to-self connections	Doing math using everyday experiences and concepts	Children's everyday activities and routines should be used to introduce and develop important civic ideas.	Meeting students' cultural norms and everyday experiences. Science learning is enhanced when the learner perceives its relevance to them.	Extend

Sources for examples in Table 9.1: Literacy Learning Strategies (Duke & Pearson, 2002); Math Learning Strategies (Anthony & Walshaw, 2009); Social Studies Learning Strategies (NCSS, 2016); Science Learning Strategies (National Research Council, 2007)

Chapter Take-Aways

This chapter provided instructional strategies that can be used to help facilitate learning through and with technology tools.

- Effective technology integration is only as good as the instructional practices used within and around the tool.

- Teachers should seek out ways to bring in strong instructional practices, such as modeling, guided practice, co-engagement, Visual Thinking strategies, and reflective practices when using technology tools.

Chapter 10

Evaluating Software for Learning

CHAPTERS 4, 5, AND 6 highlight some technology apps and websites that fit the definition of providing engaged, enhanced, or extended learning. As previously mentioned, technology in learning is only as good as the instructional strategies built around the software. However, there are digital tools with effective teaching strategies built into the software, and those tools tend to have more flexibility for generating positive learning goals when implemented with thoughtful instructional measures. Consequently, teachers should be critical while looking for software so that the technology they choose integrates the instructional practices proven to have positive outcomes on learning.

In the app stores and online, there are well over a million apps and websites that could be used for teaching and learning. Some of this software is specifically labeled for educational use while others are for general use that can be adapted for classroom instruction. Despite the educational label on many pieces of software, research has shown 77% of apps labeled for "education" have little to no empirical research that the tool will have a positive effect on learning outcomes (Vaala et al., 2015). Most teachers do not have the time to sort through the tools to find the resources that work for their curriculum. Consequently, using the Triple E Framework as a guide can be helpful in quickly evaluating software for potentially positive learning results.

In the next section, I've included an example of how the Triple E Framework can be used to evaluate both educational and non-educational software to look for effective teaching strategies built into the tool itself. We use the same Triple E measurement questions, but we change the first word from "Can" to "Does." Thus, for the first question in the engagement component, we ask, *Can the technology help students focus on the learning goals?* When we evaluate tools for potential opportunities for learning to occur, we ask, Can this tool provide opportunities to help students engage in learning goals (understanding that teachers may have to add their own supports outside of the tool)?

Evaluation of a Tool Using the Triple E Framework

We will use the Triple E Framework to evaluate Write About (writeabout.com), a web-based collaborative writing platform built to help students develop their writing process. It is set up so that teachers can synchronously annotate students' writing as they work or provide feedback (via text, image, and audio) during the writing process. Students can collaborate on writing, critique peer writing, and share their writing publicly, and parents (or other experts) can join in on the writing process with their children. Write About also includes writing prompts and ideas to help students get started on writing or to support students' own interests in writing.

For each component in the framework, we've answered "Yes" if it is actually present in the tool, "Somewhat" if it is sort of present but the teacher has to provide many instructional supports, or "No" if it is not present and it would be very difficult to provide instructional supports to make the learning effective through the tool. Table 10.1 looks at the engagement component, Table 10.2 considers the enhancement component, and Table 10.3 reviews the extension component.

Table 10.1 Assessing the Level of Engagement in Write About

Engagement in the Learning	0=No	1=Somewhat	2=Yes
1. Can the technology tool help students focus on the assignment or activity with less distraction? (time-on-task)			2
2. Can the technology tool help motivate students to begin the learning process?			2
3. Can the technology cause a shift in the behavior of the students, where they go from being passive to active social learners? (co-use)			2

Q1. Yes. The focus of Write About is on the process of learning to write, edit, and revise—not on the final product. Time is on task. Students can look at models of other students' work to see various types of writing. The teacher can and should also monitor learning by synchronously annotating students' work as they are writing. The teacher should also model how to use the tool with guided practice.

Q2. Yes. Write About includes writing prompts and scaffolds to support writing around students' interests. Write About allows the teacher to clearly identify the task and learning goal for each student.

Q3. Yes. Write About is set up for co-use so that peer and mentors can collaborate on writing together in real time. They can participate easily in share-alouds and switcheroos through the software.

Engagement Total: *6/6 points.* Write About has strong characteristics of effective engagement. The software has built-in co-engagement (through synchronous feed-back), which provides teachers opportunities to help students focus on the task of active editing and revision in the writing process. It is imperative that teachers still integrate good instructional practices, such as modeling through guided practice how to not only navigate Write About, but also how to "think" about writing when using the tool. For example, using an "I do, we do, you do" model can be an effective way to introduce the writing process in Write About. The teachers should remind students to focus on the writing task and not on how long it takes to complete the task (e.g., no awards or stickers for the first one done). Students should also be encouraged not only to collaborate within the tool with their teacher, but also to periodically stop using the technology and turn and talk to their peers and teachers, to discuss what they are doing and how they are thinking about writing.

Table 10.2 Assessing the Level of Enhancement in Write About

Enhancement of the Learning Goals	0=No	1=Somewhat	2=Yes
1. Can the technology tool allow students to develop a more sophisticated understanding of the learning goals or content? (higher-order thinking skills)			2
2. Can the technology create scaffolds to make it easier to understand concepts or ideas?			2
3. Can the technology create paths for students to demonstrate their understanding of the learning goals in a way that they could not do with traditional tools?			2

Q1.   Yes. Write About focuses on the creative process of learning to write, edit, and revise—not just on consuming information or publishing a final product. Teachers can weigh in with questions to probe for reflection as well as ask students to create their own questions for peer-to-peer feedback in the tool.

Q2.   Yes. Write About includes a selection of writing prompts (called IDEAS) for support. This allows students to choose a "just right" prompt and work at their own comfort level in the tool. In addition, the fact that teachers or other experts can collaborate on the writing process allows teachers opportunities to differentiate instruction.

Q3. Yes. While students could write, edit, and revise with paper and pencil, the ability for experts to weigh in from a distance is unique to Write About. In addition, the ability for the teacher to edit and provide feedback in real time is also something that is much more difficult to do in a traditional classroom.

Enhancement Total: *6/6 points.* Write About has strong enhancement features. With its selection of writing prompts (IDEAS) and a way for teachers and experts to weigh in on student writing in real time, Write About has the potential to enhance the learning experience. As with engagement, it is important that teachers use effective instructional strategies to encourage the enhancement. For example, teachers should mindfully differentiate writing prompts based on students' interests and writing or reading levels. Teachers should also model how to select a "just right" writing prompt in the tool, and they could encourage co-construction of ideas as well as creation of new ideas through the wide selection of writing prompts.

Table 10.3 Assessing the Level of Extension in Write About

Extension of the Learning Goals	0=No	1=Somewhat	2=Yes
1. Can the technology create opportunities for students to learn outside of their typical school day?		1	
2. Can the technology create a bridge between students' school learning and their everyday life experiences?		1	
3. Can the technology allow students to develop skills that they can use in their everyday lives?		1	

Q1. Somewhat. While the tool could be used through any digital device (mobile or stand-alone), the teacher would have to be the one to help find reasons for students to use it 24/7.

Q2. Somewhat. Write About allows experts to weigh in on the writing (if prompted by the teacher). It also allows students to publish their work to the larger internet. However, the connections need to be facilitated by the teacher; they are not intuitive in the tool.

Q3.   Somewhat. Learning how to write (digitally and analog) and understanding the process of brainstorming, editing, and revision are important soft skills for communication in society today. At the same time, most of these skills could be learned without technology tools, on pen and paper.

Extension Total: *3/6 points*. While Write About is not as strong at the extension level, it definitely provides opportunities for teachers to create extensions. With Write About, students can publish their work to a larger audience and can also take on writing prompts that are better connected to their everyday life experiences. Experts in writing (such as editors) could be invited into the tool to share their feedback on the students' writing. Thus, the teacher plays a large role in helping to make extension connections when using Write About.

TOTAL POINTS: *15/18 points*. When considering the total number of points, Write About has the potential to be beneficial for learning. The word "potential" is included because it really is important to remember that the pedagogical strategies, structures, and moves that the teacher creates around the software are key to successful learning outcomes.

It is imperative to note that while a piece of "drill and practice" software may not score very high on the Triple E Framework, it could still be integrated in a way that leads to positive learning gains. It just means that the teacher has a lot more work to do on his or her end to create structures around the tool that lead to experiences that are less "drill and practice" and more constructive, collaborative, and authentic to the learner. For example, a piece of math software that only has quizzes with multiple-choice questions that are timed as students go may not result in positive learning gains for most students. However, the teacher could change the "drill and practice" approach by pairing students up (co-use), modeling how to use the tool with an "I do, we do, you do" approach, taking away the timers and focusing on the process of doing math, monitoring use, allowing students to participate in reflective thinking activities as they go, and creating class discussions on how the problems could be authentic to their own lives.

Online Resources

Over the past decade some online resources have emerged to offer educators a way to easily search for apps and websites to use in their classroom teaching. In addition, some sites offer reviews from other educators about the potential use of the tool. While these sites are relatively new, they offer teachers a starting point to search for digital tools to use in their classroom in order to meet their learning goals. While the reviews are a starting point, I highly recommend using the Triple E Framework in addition to any review on the websites. Here are some sites that offer peer reviews on educational and general software.

Children's Technology Review Exchange (CTREX)

The Children's Technology Review Exchange (reviews.childrenstech.com) is a web and print-based publication that is designed to help both parents and teachers find media resources to help children learn. There is a very small subscription fee, but the fee is worth the detailed knowledge you get from each review. Each resource is reviewed and rated by educators. The reviews are based on an underlying theoretical framework that includes the following considerations:

- What does the child walk away from the experience(s) with that he/she didn't have at the beginning of the experience(s)?

- How does the experience empower (or disempower) a child?

- Does this experience leverage the potential of technology in a way that traditional, non-digital, or non-linear experiences cannot?

- How does this product compare with similar products?

Common Sense Education

Common Sense Education (commonsense.org/education) has a portion of its website dedicated to crowd-sourced reviews from educators who use digital resources. This website includes reviews of websites, video games, apps, and other types of software.

It also offers a "Common Core Explorer" tool, allowing teachers to plug in the Common Core State Standards (CCSS) and find digital apps and websites that meet those learning goals. (Note: Just because the software developer says the tool meets the standards, it does not necessarily mean it will. It is important for the teacher to integrate the Triple E Framework as part of the lesson planning with that tool). In addition, there is a Lesson Library, with thousands of lesson plans that integrate technology based on the CCSS. Teachers can use and/or modify these lessons, but once again, when evaluating a lesson, they need to make sure it is meeting the Triple E Framework and not just using technology as a gimmick.

EdSurge

EdSurge (edsurge.com/product-reviews) offers a product database where teachers can search by category (e.g., math, assessment, management), cost, and type of platform. While not as robust as Common Sense Education, it is a nice starting place for teachers who are looking for something that is strategy-based, not standards- or curriculum-based.

edshelf

edshelf (edshelf.com) offers a large database of tools made for teaching and learning. Teachers can search by cost, platform type, age level, subject area, keywords, and category. Similar to listings on Common Sense Education,, many tools on edshelf come with reviews from educators. The reviews are all crowd sourced, which means that anyone can log in to create a review rather than the site hiring specific teachers to create them. Thus, be aware that not all reviews are created the same or with the same critical eye.

Chapter Take-Aways

In this chapter, we used the Triple E Framework to evaluate Write About, a web-based collaborative writing platform designed to help students develop their writing process. The chapter also included online resources that teachers can use to search for digital tools they can integrate in their classroom to help students meet learning goals.

- Apps labeled for education do not necessary have any research to show they are effective for learning.

- Look for digital apps and websites that can meet the three components of the Triple E Framework (engage, enhance, and extend learning).

- Be a critical consumer of technology tools. Look for tools that are created by educators and that have strong instructional practices built into them. They should allow opportunities for students to use higher-order thinking, collaborate, and connect with authentic contexts or tasks.

- If tools do not have instructional practices built into them, then it is an opportunity to reevaluate the use of the tool or create pedagogical approaches around the tool that help meet student learning needs.

Appendix A
Lesson Planning Template Based on the Framework

WHILE HAVING A FRAMEWORK IS USEFUL, being able to put the framework into an instructional design template can be extremely practical and beneficial to the classroom teacher. This chapter provides a lesson-plan template specifically designed with the Triple E Framework and good instructional practices in mind. In order to develop a full reflective practice when using technology tools, teachers or schools may find this lesson planning template useful. It offers a complete picture of how to think about the impact of technology on the learning goals in your lesson. The planning template is extensive and is not a tool that teachers need to use all the time, but it is a great resource for professional development workshops and for beginning teachers using technology. It moves through the various aspects of the Triple E Framework in relation to the larger lesson. This planning template works with any grade or content area.

You can access the entire blank lesson planning template on the Triple E Website at www.tripleeframework.com/lesson-planning-template.html. In addition, the website includes a completed sample template to help educators understand how to complete the template.

Example Lesson Plan

Lesson Title: Air Time! Mathematical Slopes

Grade Level: Grade 8

Subject: Math

Time frame: 170 minutes (3 or 4 class periods)

Overview of Learning Goals

Content-Specific Goals	How Goals Are Met
CCSS.MATH.CONTENT.8.EE.B.5: Graph proportional relationships, interpreting the unit rate as the slope of the graph. Compare two different proportional relationships represented in different ways. For example, compare a distance-time graph to a distance-time equation to determine which of two moving objects has greater speed. **CCSS.MATH.CONTENT.8.EE.B.6:** Use similar triangles to explain why the slope m is the same between any two distinct points on a non-vertical line in the coordinate plane; derive the equation $y = mx$ for a line through the origin and the equation $y = mx + b$ for a line intercepting the vertical axis at b.	Students will watch and reflect on a BrainPOP video to understand how to calculate slope (using prior knowledge of calculating speed and distance as well). Students will graph and calculate (in Collabrify Flipbook) the slope of half-pipes and predict the speed, distance, and air time. Students will calculate the slope of half-pipes at different places on the non-linear axis to understand that slope m is in fact the same at any space. Students will research and design a skateboarding half-pipe based on a specific air time and distance criteria.
Technology-Based Goals (ISTE Student Standards)	**How Goals Are Met**
Empowered Learner (EL): Students leverage technology to take an active role in choosing, achieving, and demonstrating competency in their learning goals, informed by the learning sciences. **Knowledge Constructor (KC):** Students critically curate a variety of resources using digital tools to construct knowledge, produce creative artifacts, and make meaningful learning experiences for themselves and others. **Innovative Designer (ID):** Students use a variety of technologies within a design process to identify and solve problems by creating new, useful or imaginative solutions. **Global Collaborator (GC):** Students use digital tools to broaden their perspectives and enrich their learning by collaborating with others and working effectively in teams locally and globally.	ELs, KCs, and IDs will use the internet to gather information to design and build their own half-pipe ELs, KCs, and IDs will use a camera to capture half-pipe images and video to construct their knowledge of the relationship between slope, distance, and speed. GCs will use Collabrify Flipbook to connect with other students, the teacher, and an expert engineer around their half-pipe design.
Other Goals	**How Goals Are Met**
Learn how to perform at least two skateboarding tricks: www.exploratorium.edu/skateboarding/largeglossary.html	Students will use their newly built half-pipe to try a few tricks!

Materials Needed for Lesson

Below are technology tools and other materials to use in this lesson.

- BrainPOP (www.brainpop.com/math/algebra/slopeandintercept)

- Collabrify Flipbook Software (free) (www.imlc.io/apps)

- Camera (still and video)

- Google Customized Search Engine (cse.google.com)

- Materials (such as wood) and tools to construct a half-pipe

Lesson Overview

Share how the activities in the lesson will help meet the learning goals. How will technology play a role in meeting the learning goals?

In order to understand slopes in everyday life and their relation to speed and distance, students will learn how to calculate the slope of a skateboarding half-pipe and create their own half-pipe according to specific criteria on slope, speed, and distance. The students already know how to calculate speed and distance but not slope. They will begin the lesson by watching a short video of skateboarder Tony Hawk. The teacher will start and stop the video as he is just about to exit the half-pipe and then ask students to predict how much air time he will get as he comes off the half-pipe. The class will repeat this exercise with three or four different Tony Hawk videos until students begin to see how slopes are related to speed and distance.

Next, the students will watch a short video from BrainPOP to learn how to calculate slope. While watching the video, the students will each take notes on the Collabrify Flipbook app to show that they understand slope calculation. The students will then take a field trip to the local skateboarding park, where they will take pictures of half-pipes and calculate the slopes. They will make predictions based on their calculations as to which half-pipes will provide the most air time and speed.

Finally, they will videotape themselves going down the half-pipes and calculate the air time and speed by watching the recording. They will capture all their work in the Collabrify Flipbook app. Next the students will use pre-determined websites (identified by the teacher using Google Customized Search Engine) to research and build their own skateboarding half-pipe. They will post their research on a private Collabrify Flipbook, in which an engineer from the University of Michigan will weigh in to give them advice on their research and design ideas. They will build the half-pipe (to create a predetermined level of air time and speed) and then test it by measuring their own air time and speed on their new creation. In addition, the students will learn at least two new skateboarding tricks.

Triple E Framework Considerations

Share which technology tools you plan to integrate into the lesson. Describe how each tool will help meet your learning goals. In addition, share the instructional practices that you plan to develop in conjunction with the tool to optimize the learning.

Tool #1 BrainPOP Website

Learning goal(s) met by using the tool	Students will watch the video on how to calculate slope via skate-boarding half-pipes and complete the related activities. As a reflective practice, they will take notes on a Collabrify Flipbook to show their learnings from the video. This activity will help them understand how to calculate slope. Using a video, the students can self-pace, and there are no games or rewards at the end of the video to distract the student from the learning goals.
Is the tool integrated via teams, pairs, the individual, or other?	Individual
What features of the technology tool have elements of engagement? Answer the Triple E Engagement questions concerning how technology can bring about co-use, time-on-task learning, and focus on the learning goals. Anywhere there is a lower score (less than 4), consider adding in instructional moves in the notes to help push up the score!	Can the technology allow students to focus on the assignment/learning with less distraction (time-on-task)? No=0, **Somewhat=1**, Yes=2 Can the technology motivate students to begin the learning process? No=0, **Somewhat=1**, Yes=2 Can the technology cause a shift in behavior, from more passive to active social learners (co-use)? **No=0**, Somewhat=1, Yes=2 Score=2/6 Notes: There are few engaging pieces built into this software. It is mostly a video they watch with a few drill and practice questions. The teacher will give a software tour of how to navigate and think when using the video and completing the activities. The teacher will periodically stop and ask students to share-aloud their learning. Finally, each student will be taking notes and reflecting on their learning in their own Collabrify Flipbook that the teacher will be monitoring and weighing in on as needed. Teaching moves included (from list below): The teacher will conduct a software tour of how to use and start and stop the video. Included in the tour will be modeling of how to think about the content that is being presented and write down notes and post into Flipbook. She will model how to self-reflect on their notes. The teacher will walk around the room and monitor the students working alone. The teacher will ask the students to periodically pause and share-aloud their thinking and understanding.

Continued

Which teaching moves could be integrated to aid technology by engaging students in the learning goals?	☐ Guided practice ☑ Modeling thinking ☑ Modeling navigation of the tool ☑ Software tour ☐ I do, we do, you do ☑ Teacher monitoring ☑ Student self-reflective monitoring ☐ Co-use or co-engagement ☐ Purposeful partnering ☐ Gradual release of learning ☐ Create a mentor text ☑ Share-aloud ☐ Turn and talk ☐ Switcheroo ☐ Other
Which features of the technology tool help enhance student learning? Answer the Triple E Enhancement questions concerning how technology can bring about learning supports/scaffolds, higher-order thinking, and value added over traditional tools. Anywhere there is a lower score (less than 4), consider adding in instructional moves in the notes to help push up the score!	Can the technology allow students to develop or demonstrate a more sophisticated understanding of the learning goals (possibly use higher-order thinking skills)? **No=0**, Somewhat=1, Yes=2 Can the technology create or provide supports (scaffolds) to make it easier to understand concepts or ideas (possibly differentiate or personalize)? No=0, **Somewhat=1**, Yes=2 Can the technology create paths for students to demonstrate their understanding of the learning goals in ways they could not do with traditional tools? No=0, **Somewhat=1**, Yes=2 Score=2/6 Notes: The video allows students to have a visual of what they will be measuring at the skate park. It also permits students to start and stop the video so they can work at their own pace as they analyze the relationship between the half-pipe and slopes. This could allow for differentiation of learning. Teaching moves included (from list below): The teacher will ask students to share-aloud what they are learning as they watch the video. This will help to elicit reflective thinking and make their ideas visible. Students will be able to self-pace for differentiation of learning.

Continued

Which teaching moves could be integrated to aid technology in enhancing the learning goals?	☐ Active listening ☐ Switcheroo ☐ Self-reflective practices ☐ Visible Thinking routines ☐ Graphic organizers ☐ Visual representations of learning ☐ Reflective notebooks ☐ Anticipation guides ☐ Questioning practices ☐ Predicting ☑ Differentiation ☐ Personalization ☑ Share-aloud ☐ Other
How does the technology extend the learning goals? Answer the Triple E Extend questions concerning how technology can bring about learning that connects to everyday life, allows learners to continue to learn 24/7, and helps them develop soft skills. Anywhere there is a lower score (less than 4), consider adding in instructional moves in the notes to help push up the score!	Can the technology create opportunities for the students to learn outside the typical school day? No=0, **Somewhat=1**, Yes=2 Can the technology create a bridge between school learning and everyday life (authentic experiences)? No=0, Somewhat=1, **Yes=2** Can the technology allow students to build authentic life skills, which they can use in their everyday life (soft skills)? No=0, **Somewhat=1**, Yes=2 Score=1/6 Notes: The video is discussing how to measure slope based on an actual half-pipe, which helps connect to their authentic problem that they are addressing. Yet the video is a cartoon and not very authentic for developing soft skills or creating new opportunities to learn outside their school day. Teaching moves included (from list below): The teacher will be using a real-world problem that the students will investigate.

Continued

Which teaching moves could be integrated to aid technology in extending the learning goals?	☑ Real-world issues ☐ Partner with real-world organizations ☐ Connect with authentic experts ☐ Engage students in authentic discourse with others ☐ Pen pals ☐ Students investigate and direct their own project ☐ Role-playing ☐ Use authentic tools that are prominent in everyday life ☐ Other
Lesson Setup How will you prepare to use this piece of technology in the lesson? What do you need to do to get the technology ready? • Selecting the "just right" tool or part of the resource • Setting up accounts • Differentiating • Personalizing • Creating models or mentor	Student accounts should be created in advance in BrainPOP, so they can easily login and get started without distraction. The teacher may want to pre-plan a note-taking template for the video (at least for students who may need this support).
Assessment How will you assess the activities happening through the tool? • Monitoring/observation • Formative assessment • Informal assessment • Summative assessment	The teacher will conduct assessment by monitoring the students as they are watching the video. In addition, the teacher will ask the students to take notes and share them via Collabrify Flipbook. The teacher can monitor the note-taking to make certain they understand how to properly calculate slope.

Tool #2 Still and Video Camera

Learning goal(s) met by using the tool	Students will take pictures of the half-pipes at the skate park and then use a ruler or draw on them to calculate the slope. They will also be able to predict the air time and speed that their chosen team member will end up going down the half-pipe. They will meet both their math learning goals by calculating the slope, but also be able to determine that the slope m is the same at each point along the slope on the non-vertical line. They will use the video camera to take video of their team members going down the half-pipe. They will calculate the air time and speed. They will compare how close they were in their speed and air time calculation. They will also be able to make inferences about the different angles of a slope and speed/air time.
Is the tool integrated via teams, pairs, the individual, or other?	Teams
Which features of the technology tool support engagement? Answer the Triple E Engagement questions concerning how technology can bring about co-use, time-on-task learning, and focus on the learning goals. Anywhere there is a lower score (less than 4), consider adding in instructional moves in the notes to help push up the score!	Can the technology allow students to focus on the assignment/learning with less distraction (time-on-task)? No=0, **Somewhat=1**, Yes=2 Can the technology motivate students to begin the learning process? No=0, **Somewhat=1**, Yes=2 Can the technology cause a shift in behavior, from more passive to active social learners (co-use)? No=0, **Somewhat=1**, Yes=2 Score=3/6 Notes: There are few engaging pieces built into the tool. The teacher will need to model "how to" think about capturing the slope so that it can be measured in a picture as well as on video. The teacher can do this through an "I do, we do, you do" approach at the skate park. The students will be co-using the cameras in teams. The teams will be reporting and sharing their work and conclusions via the team Collabrify Flipbook. Teaching moves included (from list below): The teacher will model how to use the camera to shoot the video and still pictures. Then the teacher will model what they should be noticing and paying attention to in their filming. The teacher will model using an "I do, we do, you do" approach. The students will co-engage in the technology by working in teams. The teacher will walk around and monitor teams as they work.

Continued

Which teaching moves could be integrated to aid technology by engaging students in the learning goals?	☐ Guided practice ☑ Modeling thinking ☐ Modeling navigation of the tool ☐ Software tour ☑ I do, we do, you do ☑ Teacher monitoring ☐ Student self-reflective monitoring ☑ Co-use or co-engagement ☐ Purposeful partnering ☐ Gradual release of learning ☑ Create a mentor text ☐ Share-aloud ☐ Turn and talk ☐ Switcheroo ☐ Other
Which features of the technology tool enhance student learning? Answer the Triple E Enhancement questions concerning how technology can bring about learning supports/scaffolds, higher-order thinking, and value added over traditional tools. Anywhere there is a lower score (less than 4), consider adding in instructional moves in the notes to help push up the score!	Can the technology allow students to develop or demonstrate a more sophisticated understanding of the learning goals (possibly use higher-order thinking skills)? No=0, **Somewhat=1**, Yes=2 Can the technology create or provide supports (scaffolds) to make it easier to understand concepts or ideas (possibly differentiate or personalize)? No=0, **Somewhat=1**, Yes=2 Can the technology create paths for students to demonstrate their understanding of the learning goals in ways they could not do with traditional tools? No=0, Somewhat=1, Yes=2 Score=2/6 Notes: The added value of the camera is that it captures the video in the moment and will allow for playback so that the speed can be measured. In addition, the still images of the slope make the slope easier to measure as a two-dimensional object. Teaching moves included (from list below): The teacher will ask the students to predict what will happen prior to filming. They will be given an anticipation guide to help them think through their predictions and the actual results.

Continued

Which teaching moves could be integrated to aid technology in enhancing the learning goals?	☐ Active listening ☐ Switcheroo ☐ Self-reflective practices ☐ Visible Thinking routines ☐ Graphic organizers ☐ Visual representations of learning ☐ Reflective notebooks ☑ Anticipation guides ☐ Questioning practices ☑ Predicting ☐ Differentiation ☐ Personalization ☐ Share-aloud ☐ Other
How does the technology extend the learning goals? Answer the Triple E Extend questions concerning how technology can bring about learning that connects to everyday life, allows learners to continue to learn 24/7, and helps them develop soft skills. Anywhere there is a lower score (less than 4), consider adding in instructional moves in the notes to help push up the score!	Can the technology create opportunities for the students to learn outside the typical school day? No=0, **Somewhat=1**, Yes=2 Can the technology create a bridge between school learning and everyday life (authentic experiences)? No=0, Somewhat=1, **Yes=2** Can the technology allow students to build authentic life skills, which they can use in their everyday lives (soft skills)? No=0, **Somewhat=1**, Yes=2 Score=4/6 Notes: The camera allows students to capture skateboarding in real life and can slow down the skateboarding so that they can measure the authentic example. This helps students understand how to use video to capture and measure real world experiences. Teaching moves included (from list below): The teacher will be using a real-world problem that the students will investigate. The students will also be using their own video cameras on their mobile devices.

Continued

Which teaching moves could be integrated to aid technology in extending the learning goals?	☑ Real-world issues ☐ Partner with real-world organizations ☐ Connect with authentic experts ☐ Engage students in authentic discourse with others ☐ Pen pals ☐ Students investigate and direct their own project ☐ Role-playing ☑ Use authentic tools that are prominent in everyday life ☐ Other
Lesson Setup How will you prepare to use this piece of technology in the lesson? What do you need to do to get the technology ready? • Selecting the "just right" tool or part of the resource • Setting up accounts • Differentiating • Personalizing • Creating models or mentor	Make certain that each team has a camera that can capture still images and at least 30 seconds of video.
Assessment How will you assess the activities happening through the tool? • Monitoring/observation • Formative assessment • Informal assessment • Summative assessment	The teacher will be observing and monitoring the teams' activities with the camera. In addition, each team will post their findings on their collaborative Collabrify Flipbook, which the teacher can also use to monitor posts and provide feedback.

Tool #3 Internet Search Engines (Google Customized Search Engine)

Learning goal(s) met by using the tool	The students will use the customized search engine (created by the teacher to pre-select websites that are authoritative and on-task) to research how to create a half-pipe and how to make it according to the air time and speed specifications set by the teacher.
Is the tool integrated via teams, pairs, the individual, or other?	Teams
Which features of the technology tool support engagement? Answer the Triple E Engagement questions concerning how technology can bring about co-use, time-on-task learning, and focus on the learning goals. Anywhere there is a lower score (less than 4), consider adding in instructional moves in the notes to help push up the score!	Can the technology allow students to focus on the assignment/learning with less distraction (time-on-task)? No=0, **Somewhat=1**, Yes=2 Can the technology motivate students to begin the learning process? No=0, **Somewhat=1**, Yes=2 Can the technology cause a shift in behavior, from more passive to active social learners (co-use)? **No=0**, Somewhat=1, Yes=2 Score=2/6 Notes: There are few engaging pieces built into the tool. The teacher will show the teams how to navigate the search engine and ask them to brainstorm as a group what they should be looking for. The teacher will develop a mentor text Collabrify Flipbook so they can understand how to begin to organize their thinking. Periodically, the teacher should ask the teams to share what they are learning and their progress with the other teams. The students will be co-constructing knowledge together in their teams. Teaching moves included (from list below): The teacher will demonstrate through guided practice how to do a custom search using the search engine, and posting notes into their Flipbook notebooks. The teacher will create a mentor text (example) as part of the guided practice. The students will work in their teams (co-use) as they search. The teacher will ask the teams to periodically pause and share-aloud their thinking and understanding.

Continued

Which teaching moves could be integrated to aid technology by engaging students in the learning goals?	☑ Guided practice ☐ Modeling thinking ☐ Modeling navigation of the tool ☐ Software tour ☐ I do, we do, you do ☐ Teacher monitoring ☐ Student self-reflective monitoring ☑ Co-use or co-engagement ☐ Purposeful partnering ☐ Gradual release of learning ☑ Create a mentor text ☑ Share-aloud ☐ Turn and talk ☐ Switcheroo ☐ Other
Which features of the technology tool enhance student learning? Answer the Triple E Enhancement questions concerning how technology can bring about learning supports/scaffolds, higher-order thinking, and value added over traditional tools. Anywhere there is a lower score (less than 4), consider adding in instructional moves in the notes to help push up the score!	Can the technology allow students to develop or demonstrate a more sophisticated understanding of the learning goals (possibly use higher-order thinking skills)? No=0, Somewhat=1, Yes=2 Can the technology create or provide supports (scaffolds) to make it easier to understand concepts or ideas (possibly differentiate or personalize)? No=0, Somewhat=1, **Yes=2** Can the technology create paths for students to demonstrate their understanding of the learning goals in ways they could not do with traditional tools? No=0, **Somewhat=1**, Yes=2 Score=3/6 Notes: The customized search engine provides options for students of different learning and reading levels to get similar information. They will be able to learn how to construct their half-pipe by using the Internet resources. Teaching moves included (from list below): The students will organize their notes in a graphic organizer with Collabrify Flipbook as they are researching. This will also serve as a research notebook. They will periodically be sharing aloud what they are learning and using evidence from their Flipbook to support their ideas. The custom search engine will have different reading levels to choose from, so students can locate articles and research for their "just right" reading level.

Continued

Which teaching moves could be integrated to aid technology in enhancing the learning goals?	☐ Active listening ☐ Switcheroo ☐ Self-reflective practices ☐ Visible Thinking routines ☑ Graphic organizers ☐ Visual representations of learning ☑ Reflective notebooks ☐ Anticipation guides ☐ Questioning practices ☐ Predicting ☑ Differentiation ☐ Personalization ☑ Share-aloud ☐ Other
How does the technology extend the learning goals? Answer the Triple E Extend questions concerning how technology can bring about learning that connects to everyday life, allows learners to continue to learn 24/7, and helps them develop soft skills. Anywhere there is a lower score (less than 4), consider adding in instructional moves in the notes to help push up the score!	Can the technology create opportunities for the students to learn outside the typical school day? No=0, **Somewhat=1**, Yes=2 Can the technology create a bridge between school learning and everyday life (authentic experiences)? **No=0**, Somewhat=1, Yes=2 Can the technology allow students to build authentic life skills, which they can use in their everyday lives (soft skills)? No=0, **Somewhat=1**, Yes=2 Score=2/6 Notes: The custom Google search engine does not organically extend learning or build a bridge between school learning and everyday life experiences. However, there are some soft skills that come into play, including students using their inquiry skills to ask questions and gather evidence from authoritative resources to provide evidence for how to properly construct their half-pipe. This could be transferred to searching for other things they would like to do in their everyday lives. Teaching moves included (from list below): The teacher will be using a real-world problem that the students will investigate, as well as model investigative strategies using the custom search engine. The teacher will also discuss the significance of authoritative resources when researching online (soft skills).

Continued

Which teaching moves could be integrated to aid technology in extending the learning goals?	☑ Real-world issues ☐ Partner with real-world organizations ☐ Connect with authentic experts ☐ Engage students in authentic discourse with others ☐ Pen pals ☑ Students investigate and direct their own project ☐ Role-playing ☐ Use authentic tools that are prominent in everyday life ☐ Other
Lesson Setup How will you prepare to use this piece of technology in the lesson? What do you need to do to get the technology ready? • Selecting the "just right" tool or part of the resource • Setting up accounts • Differentiating • Personalizing • Creating models or mentor	Teacher should set up the Google custom search engine and make the URL tiny so the link is easy for the students to access.
Assessment How will you assess the activities happening through the tool? • Monitoring/observation • Formative assessment • Informal assessment • Summative assessment	The teacher and an engineer will be observing and monitoring the teams' activities and research choices in Collabrify Flipbook. In addition, the teacher will be evaluating the final half-pipe that the students construct to see if it meets the assignment criteria.

Tool #4 Collabrify Flipbook

Learning goal(s) met by using the tool	Collabrify Flipbook will be used throughout this lesson. This technology serves as a reflective tool because the students can take notes individually as they watch the BrainPOP video. Collabrify Flipbook also lets the teacher weigh in and comment as the students are taking notes and sketching out their mathematical formulas. This gives the teacher an opportunity to synchronously monitor the student learning and co-engage in the learning process as students demonstrate how to calculate slope from the video. It would be much more difficult to collect individual notes on paper. The students can share their research on a Collabrify Flipbook, which lets them collaborate with their team members while also allowing the teacher and an expert from the University of Michigan to weigh in on their work throughout the activity.
Is the tool integrated via teams, pairs, the individual, or other?	Teams
Which features of the technology tool support engagement? Answer the Triple E Engagement questions concerning how technology can bring about co-use, time-on-task learning, and focus on the learning goals. Anywhere there is a lower score (less than 4), consider adding in instructional moves in the notes to help push up the score!	Can the technology allow students to focus on the assignment/learning with less distraction (time-on-task)? No=0, Somewhat=1, **Yes=2** Can the technology motivate students to begin the learning process? No=0, Somewhat=1, **Yes=2** Can the technology cause a shift in behavior, from more passive to active social learners (co-use)? No=0, Somewhat=1, **Yes=2** Score=6/6 **Notes:** Collabrify Flipbook has real-time collaboration built into it. Beyond using text, Collabrify Flipbook allows students to draw and sketch out ideas, and the software is made for synchronous collaborative use, thus other students, teachers, and experts can also type and draw on the document in real time. In addition, it has few distractions from the text of the document. The students will also either be co-using the document by working in teams or connecting with the teacher or an expert engineer through Collabrify Flipbook sharing options. **Teaching moves included (from list below):** The teacher will conduct a software tour of how to use Collabrify Flipbook. Included in the tour will be modeling and navigation of the tool. In addition, they will create a mentor text together as part of the software tour. Students will be working in teams so that they co-use the software (in addition to co-engaging through the software's collaborative features). Finally, teams will participate in a switcheroo, where they will take over another team's Flipbook to give them constructive feedback.

Continued

Which teaching moves could be integrated to aid technology by engaging students in the learning goals?	☐ Guided practice ☑ Modeling thinking ☑ Modeling navigation of the tool ☑ Software tour ☐ I do, we do, you do ☐ Teacher monitoring ☐ Student self-reflective monitoring ☑ Co-use or co-engagement ☐ Purposeful partnering ☐ Gradual release of learning ☑ Create a mentor text ☐ Share-aloud ☐ Turn and talk ☑ Switcheroo ☐ Other
Which features of the technology tool enhance student learning? Answer the Triple E Enhancement questions concerning how technology can bring about learning supports/scaffolds, higher-order thinking, and value added over traditional tools. Anywhere there is a lower score (less than 4), consider adding in instructional moves in the notes to help push up the score!	Can the technology allow students to develop or demonstrate a more sophisticated understanding of the learning goals (possibly use higher-order thinking skills)? No=0, Somewhat=1, **Yes=2** Can the technology create or provide supports (scaffolds) to make it easier to understand concepts or ideas (possibly differentiate or personalize)? No=0, Somewhat=1, **Yes=2** Can the technology create paths for students to demonstrate their understanding of the learning goals in ways they could not do with traditional tools? No=0, **Somewhat=1**, Yes=2 Score=5/6 Notes: Collabrify Flipbook allows students to collaborate with other members of the class, the teacher, and an expert through the tool. Collabrify Flipbook also works in conjunction with the other Collabrify suite of tools (maps, writer, spreadsheets, etc.) so that students can use the tool that best helps them co-construct ideas. All of the tools have built-in collaboration features. Teaching moves included (from list below): The students will be working in Flipbooks and discussing ideas with the engineers as well as their peers. Flipbook already has built-in collaboration features and scaffolds.

Continued

Which teaching moves could be integrated to aid technology in enhancing the learning goals?	☐ Active listening ☐ Switcheroo ☐ Self-reflective practices ☐ Visible Thinking routines ☐ Graphic organizers ☐ Visual representations of learning ☐ Reflective notebooks ☐ Anticipation guides ☐ Questioning practices ☐ Predicting ☐ Differentiation ☐ Personalization ☐ Share-aloud ☐ Other
How does the technology extend the learning goals? Answer the Triple E Extend questions concerning how technology can bring about learning that connects to everyday life, allows learners to continue to learn 24/7, and helps them develop soft skills. Anywhere there is a lower score (less than 4), consider adding in instructional moves in the notes to help push up the score!	Can the technology create opportunities for the students to learn outside the typical school day? No=0, **Somewhat=1**, Yes=2 Can the technology create a bridge between school learning and everyday life (authentic experiences)? No=0, Somewhat=1, **Yes=2** Can the technology allow students to build authentic life skills, which they can use in their everyday lives (soft skills)? No=0, **Somewhat=1**, Yes=2 Score=4/6 Notes: Through its collaborative features, Collabrify Flipbook allows students to connect with an expert on engineering and construction. Students can use the app to engage in authentic discussions about the construction of their half-pipe. Teaching Moves Included (from list below): The teacher will be using a real-world problem, bringing in real engineers through the software, and asking students to engage in synchronous discourse with others on the development of the half-pipe.

Continued

Which teaching moves could be integrated to aid technology in extending the learning goals?	☑ Real-world issues ☐ Partner with real-world organizations ☑ Connect with authentic experts ☑ Engage students in authentic discourse with others ☐ Pen pals ☐ Students investigate and direct their own project ☐ Role-playing ☐ Use authentic tools that are prominent in everyday life ☐ Other
Lesson Setup How will you prepare to use this piece of technology in the lesson? What do you need to do to get the technology ready? • Selecting the "just right" tool or part of the resource • Setting up accounts • Differentiating • Personalizing • Creating models or mentor	Google Accounts should be set up (Collabrify Flipbook works with Google). The expert engineer should receive instructions on how to connect with the student teams.
Assessment How will you assess the activities happening through the tool? • Monitoring/observation • Formative assessment • Informal assessment • Summative assessment	The teacher and an engineer will be observing and monitoring the teams' activities in Collabrify Flipbook. In addition, the teacher will be evaluating the final half-pipe that the students construct to see if it meets the assignment criteria.

Procedures

What is the minute-to-minute activity that will be happening in the lesson? Describe what the teacher is going to do and say, as well as what the students are going to do.

Day 1 In the Classroom

Time stamp / What is the teacher's role?	What are the students going to do?	What is the teacher going to say?
0–5 Minutes: Teacher will introduce the project with a video of Tony Hawk.	Students will watch the Tony Hawk videos, make predictions, and answer the teacher's questions from direct instruction.	"Today we are going to learn how to become Tony Hawk! Watch this video, and when I stop it, I want you to predict how much air time, in seconds, Tony will get." Ask probing questions: "Why did you predict that?" "How does the half-pipe play a role in your prediction?" Let students know the end goal too: "You are going to have a chance to build your own skateboarding half-pipe!
5–7 Minutes: Teacher shows how to use BrainPOP (modeling thinking and a "we do").	Students will watch the teacher model and participate in the "we do."	"Eyes on me as I show you a software tour of BrainPOP. First, I want to show you how to log in to BrainPOP. Once you log in, you will click on the slope video. As you watch it, you will be using Collabrify Flipbook to take notes and sketch out your ideas for how to calculate the slope of a half-pipe. For example, as I watch this scene I notice that the half-pipe seems to have a steep slope, so I am going to write that down in my Flipbook notes. I am going to count the seconds that it takes the skateboarder to come down from the air. Let's count that together. It says that he went 5 feet. What did everyone get for the air time? How can we calculate the speed of how fast he went in the air? Good. Now the trick is going to be figuring out the slope. That is your task. As you watch the video, write down the equation you need to know in Flipbook. You can rewind the video or pause it. There is no rush getting through the video. I will be monitoring your work in Flipbook. Once you think you understand how to calculate the slope, try the practice quiz."

Continued

Time stamp / What is the teacher's role?	What are the students going to do?	What is the teacher going to say?
7–25 Minutes: Teacher will circulate and monitor the students as they are using BrainPOP. He/she will also be using an iPad to see the individual students' work in Flipbook.	Students get out laptops and begin to use the BrainPOP website at their own pace.	"Now it is your turn. Please get a laptop and log in to BrainPOP and Collabrify Flipbook. Please share your Flipbook with me so I can monitor your work. Begin watching the video at your own pace. I will walk around to help and check in on your work."
25–30 Minutes: Teacher will ask students to participate in a share-aloud.	Students will share what they have learned thus far about calculating slope.	"Hands off computers and eyes on me. I want you to look at your notes for 30 seconds. I want you to find two things to share that you have learned about calculating slope."
30–40 Minutes: Teacher continues to circulate and periodically sits down with students as they work.	Students will continue to work on understanding slope via the BrainPOP video and website activities, and they will continue to share ideas in Flipbook.	Teacher should ask probing and predicting questions as they sit down with different teams.
40–45 Minutes: Teacher will ask students to participate in a turn and talk.	Students will find a partner and share what they have learned about calculating slope on a half-pipe. A couple of pairs will be asked to share out.	"Hands off computers and eyes on me. I want you to look at your notes for 30 seconds. I want you to find a partner from your pre-assigned team and share how you know how to calculate slope on a half-pipe." "I will ask two teams to share out loud what they know."
45–55 Minutes: Teacher places students in teams and asks them to prepare for their field trip to the skate park the next day.	Students will get in their pre-determined teams, set up their Collabrify Flipbook for the team, share it with everyone. They will make a plan for each team member to have a role at the skate park the next day (note-taker, camera person, measurer, double-checker).	"Now it is time to get into your teams of four. Please take a minute and give everyone a role from the list on the board. Then set up your Flipbook for the team and share it with me. Decide whose cell phone camera you will use to record. It needs to be able to take a still picture and capture at least 30 seconds of video at a time. Your plan should be documented in your Flipbook."

Day 2 At the Skate Park

Time stamp / What is the teacher's role?	What are the students going to do?	What is the teacher going to say?
0–10 Minutes: Students are placed in teams and teacher explains the procedures for the day. Teacher models through guided practice how to use cameras to capture slope, and then how to calculate the slope from the image. Teacher uses "I do, we do, you do" to work with students on creating a mentor text sample of what the students will create.	Students will gather in their teams with their mobile devices. Teams should have one camera and one or two devices to document the experience with Collabrify Flipbook. They will listen to the instructions and watch the guided practice model by the teacher. Students watch the teacher model the "I do" without their devices in hand. Next, students get their cameras and do the "we do" with the teacher.	"Please get into your teams. Eyes on me as I show you how to use your camera to capture the image of a half-pipe so you can calculate the slope. You can select any of the half-pipes here at the skate park. I am going to take a picture at the side angle so I can see the slope. I want everyone to come take a look at what I mean. Now I am putting the picture into Flipbook and I will sketch out how to calculate the slope here in Flipbook. I will find the rise and the run. Now that I have found the slope, I will try to estimate the distance, speed, and air time that my chosen team member will get when he/she actually goes down the half-pipe. This is a prediction, but to make a good prediction I need to think about the slope and how it will play a role. My slope is pretty steep … what does that mean?" Students answer. "How can it help me determine my prediction?" Students answer. "Now let's do one together." Students and teacher will work on one together. "Alright, now it is your turn. Please make sure to document everything in Flipbook, where I will be monitoring your work."
10–35 Minutes: Teacher monitors teams as they document their learning in Flipbook and then circulates as teams are working at the skate park.	Students take pictures of three half-pipes and calculate the slopes. They then make predictions on which ones will have the most air time and speed. They will document their learning in Flipbook.	Teacher should ask probing and predicting type questions while circulating among different teams. Questions may include: "How did you figure out the air time?" "How did you measure the slope?" "Why is the slope important in determining the speed?"

Continued

Time stamp / What is the teacher's role?	What are the students going to do?	What is the teacher going to say?
35–45 Minutes: Teacher models how to use the video camera to record someone going down the half-pipe and how to use that video to calculate speed, distance, and time.	Students watch the teacher model, then calculate the speed, time, and distance by having someone do the half-pipe.	"Now I need a volunteer to skate down my chosen half-pipe while I videotape. Remember we predicted that the air time would be 4 seconds and the distance would be 5 feet. Let's see how accurate we are. I am going to make sure I capture the person at the edge of the half-pipe and the landing spot so I am doing a long shot. As our student goes down the half-pipe, I want everyone to count how long they are on the ramp and how long they are in the air." Now the student goes down the half-pipe while the teacher videotapes. "What did everyone get?" "So the air time was 2 seconds and the distance was 3 feet when we measure it in real time on the ground. So what is the speed? How do we calculate that?" Students share answers and they do it together. They re-watch the video to double-check their work.
45–55 Minutes: Teacher monitors teams as they document their learning in Flipbook and then circulates as teams are working at the skate park.	Students take videos of one team member going down each slope. Students then use the videos to calculate the air time and speed. They compare and contrast them, trying to understand how slope plays a role.	Teacher will circulate among the teams and ask probing questions, including: "What criteria did you use to measure the slope?" "How did you decide which slope to measure?" "What role do you think the slope played in the air time?"
55–60 Minutes: Teacher asks students to pause and turn and talk to reflect on what they are learning about the relationship between slope, speed, and distance.	Students reflect in their teams with a turn and talk and then as a share-aloud with the whole group.	"Now please take a minute to turn and talk with someone in a different team about what you know about slope, speed, and distance. Also, what do you still wonder about slope, speed, and distance? Finally, share how this will impact the building of your own half-pipe."

Day 3 In the Classroom

Time stamp / What is the teacher's role?	What are the students going to do?	What is the teacher going to say?
0–3 Minutes: Teacher introduces the goal for the day. Teacher reviews what the students learned about slope in the previous two classes.	Students listen to teacher review the goals for the day.	"Today we are going to start working on your research to build your half-pipe. Remember that you need to build a half-pipe that allows your chosen teammate to have at least 2 seconds of air time but no more than 5 seconds. In addition, you need to make sure you go at least 2 feet. You will be using the custom search engine I created to do all your research. Please notice that there are three different search engines depending on your reading level, so choose the one that is "just right" for you. Before starting your research, I want your team to brainstorm the important keywords that you need to use in order to refine your search. This brainstorm should be reflected in your Flipbook. When you use the custom search engine, you will need to put quotes around connecting words such as "half-pipe" or "slope intercept." You need to come up with materials to build your half-pipe and determine the slope of your half-pipe (provide evidence that this slope will meet the criteria)." "I will be monitoring your work in Flipbook."
3–5 Minutes: Teacher models how to use the custom search engine.	Teams work together to research how to build a half-pipe. They post their findings on Flipbook.	Teacher should ask reflective thinking questions while circulating around to different teams.
5–20 Minutes: Teacher monitors work by circulating and checking work via Flipbook.	Teams work together to research how to build a half-pipe. They post their findings on Flipbook.	Teacher should ask reflective thinking questions while circulating around to different teams.
20–30 Minutes: Teacher asks teams to do a switcheroo.	Teams each share their Flipbook with another team and begin to comment and give feedback on the other team's work.	"Time for a switcheroo. Please share your Flipbook with the team to your right. Give comments on the resources they found, the materials they selected, and how they are determining the slope. Saying 'good job' is not helpful feedback. Helpful feedback is asking probing questions or suggesting other resources."

Continued

Time stamp / What is the teacher's role?	What are the students going to do?	What is the teacher going to say?
30–50 Minutes: Teacher monitors work by circulating and checking work via Flipbook.	Teams work together to research how to build a half-pipe. They post their findings on Flipbook.	Teacher should ask reflective thinking questions while circulating around to different teams.
50–60 Minutes: Teacher tells teams how to share their research with the engineer expert. Teacher shares the building process: teams will have one week to build their half-pipe and demonstrate it the next week in class (if time allows, they could bring in materials and build during the next class). Teacher shares the rubric that will be used to assess their projects.	Teams work together to research how to build a half-pipe. They post their findings on Flipbook.	"Please share your research and two questions that you would like our expert engingeertom@umich.edu to respond to. Dr. Russell will weigh in on your work over the next week." "Next week, you will bring in your half-pipes and we will try them out! Be prepared to share a new trick that you learned on your half-pipe. We will be predicting the air time and speed!"

Appendix B

References

Angeli, C., & Valanides, N. (2009). Epistemological and methodological issues for the conceptualization, development, and assessment of ICT–TPCK: Advances in Technological Pedagogical Content Knowledge (TPCK). *Computers & Education, 52*(1), 154–168.

Anthony, G., and Walshaw, M. (2009). *Effective pedagogy in mathematics.* International Academy of Education.

Archambault, L. M., & Barnett, J. H. (2010). Revisiting technological pedagogical content knowledge: Exploring the TPACK framework. *Computers & Education, 55*(4), 1656–1662.

Barron, B., & Darling-Hammond, L. (2008). Powerful learning: Studies show deep understanding derives from collaborative methods. Retrieved from https://www.edutopia.org/inquiry-project-learning-research

Bebell, D., & O'Dwyer, L. (2010). Educational outcomes and research from 1:1 computing settings. *The Journal of Technology, Learning, and Assessment, 9*(1), 1–16. Retrieved from http://ejournals.bc.edu/ojs/index.php/jtla/article/view/1606/1463

Becker, H. J. (2000). Findings from the teaching, learning, and computing survey: Is Larry Cuban right? [PDF file]. Center for Research on Information Technology and Organizations. Retrieved from http://epaa.asu.edu/ojs/article/view/442

Beetham, H. (2007). *Rethinking pedagogy for a digital age: designing and delivering e-learning.* London; New York: Routledge.

Bell, B.S., & Kozlowski, S.W.J. (2003). Adaptive guidance: Enhancing self-regulation, knowledge, and performance in technology-based training. *Personnel Psychology. 55*(2), 267–306.

Bloom, B. (Ed.). (1956). *Taxonomy of Educational Objectives, the classification of educational goals—Handbook I: Cognitive Domain.* New York: McKay.

Brantley-Dias, L., & Ertmer, P.A. (2013). Goldilocks and TPACK: Is the Construct "Just Right?" *A Journal of Research on Technology in Education;* Winter 2013/2014; 46, 2; ProQuest Research Library pg. 103.

Brown, J. S., Collins, A., & Duguid, P. (1989). Situated cognition and the culture of learning. *Educational Researcher, 18*(1), 32–42.

Bruner, J. S. (1966) *Toward a Theory of Instruction.* Cambridge, Mass.: Belkapp Press.

Chen, P.S.D., Lambert, A.D., & Guidry, K.R. (2010). Engaging online learners: The impact of web-based technology on college student engagement. *Computers & Education, 54*(4), 1222–1232.

Conole, G., Brasher, A., Cross, S., Weller, M., Clark, P., & Culver, J. (2008). Visualising learning design to foster and support good practice and creativity. *Educational Media International, 45*(3), 177–194.

Conoley, J., Moore, G., Croom, B., & Flowers, J. (2006). A toy or a teaching tool? The use of audience-response systems in the classroom. *Techniques, 81*(7), 46–49.

Cuban, L. (2001). *Oversold and underused: Computers in the classroom.* Cambridge, MA: Harvard University Press.

Darling-Hammond, L., Zielezinksi, M.B., & Goldman, S. (2014). Using technology to support at-risk students' learning. SCOPE. Retrieved from https://edpolicy.stanford.edu/sites/default/files/scope-pub-using-technology-report.pdf

Darling-Hammond, L., Barron, B., Pearson, D.P., Schoenfeld, A.H., Stage, E.K., Zimmerman, T.D., Cervetti, G.N., Tilson, J.L., & Chen, M. (2008). Powerful learning: What we know about teaching for understanding. (1st ed.) Jossey-Bass.

Dewey, J., & Small, A. W. (1897). *My pedagogic creed* (No. 25). EL Kellogg & Company.

Diaz, D. P. & Bontenbal, K. F. (2000). Pedagogy-based technology training. In P. Hoffman & D. Lemke (Eds.), *Teaching and Learning in a Network World,* pp. 50–54. Amsterdam, Netherlands: IOS Press.

Donovan, L., Green, T., & Hartley, K. (2010). An examination of one-to-one computing in the middle school: Does increased access bring about increased student engagement? *Journal of Educational Computing Research. 42*(4), 423–441.

Duke, N.K., & Pearson, P.D. (2002). Effective practices for developing reading comprehension. In A.E. Farstrup & S.J. Samuels (Eds.), *What Research Has to Say About Reading Instruction* (3rd ed., pp. 205–242). Newark, DE: International Reading Association.

Ertmer, P.A. (1999). Addressing first- and second-order barriers to change: Strategies for technology integration. *Educational Technology Research & Development. 47*(4), 47–61.

The Partnership for 21st Century Skills. (2011). *Framework for 21st Century Learning.* [PDF file].The Partnership for 21st Century Skills. Retrieved from www.p21.org/storage/documents/1.__p21_framework_2-pager.pdf

Filer, D. (2010). Everyone's answering: Using technology to increase classroom participation. *Nursing Education Perspectives, 31*(4), 247–250.

Firek, H. (April 2003). One order of ed tech coming up ... You want fries with that? *Phi Delta Kappan, 84*(8) 596–597.

Fuchs, T., & Woessmann, L. (2004). Computers and student learning: Bivariate and multivariate evidence on the availability and use of computers at home and at school. CESifo Working Paper No. 1321. [PDF file]. Retrieved from www.cesifo-group.de/portal/pls/portal/docs/1/1188938.PDF

Graham, C. R. (2011). Theoretical Considerations for Understanding Technological Pedagogical Content Knowledge (TPACK). *Computers & Education, 57*(2011), 1953–1969.

Graham, C.R., Borup, J. and Smith, N.B. (2012), Using TPACK as a framework to understand teacher candidates' technology integration decisions. *Journal of Computer Assisted Learning, 28*(6): 530–546.

Gess-Newsome, J. (2002). Pedagogical content knowledge: An introduction and orientation. In J. Gess-Newsome & N. Lederman (Eds.), PCK and Science Education (pp. 3–17). New York, NY: Kluwer Academic Publishers.

Guernsey, L. (2012). Can your preschooler learn anything from an iPad app? Slate. Retrieved from www.lisaguernsey.com/articles&volume=1&issue=can-preschoolers-learn-anything-from-an-app

Halpern, R. (2012). It takes a whole society: Opening up the learning landscape in the high school years. Quincy, MA: Nellie Mae Education Foundation. Retrieved from www.nmefoundation.org/getmedia/747d8095-748b-4876-a3dd-ebc763796e1d/358NM-Halpern-Full

Herrington, J., Reeves, T. C. & Oliver, R. (2010). *A guide to authentic e-learning.* New York: Routledge.

Hirsh-Pasek, K., Zosh, J., Golinkoff, R.M. Gray, J., Robb, M., & Kaufman, J. (2015). Putting education in "educational" apps: Lessons from the science of learning. *Psychological Science in the Public Interest, 16*(1) 3–34.

Jimoyiannis, A. (2010). Designing and implementing an integrated technological pedagogical science knowledge framework for science teachers' professional development. *Computers & Education, 55*(3), 1259–1269.

Jonassen, D. H. (Ed.). (2004). *Handbook of research on educational communications and technology* (2nd ed.). Mahwah, NJ: Lawrence Earlbaum Associates.

Kalyuga, S. (2006). Assessment of learners' organized knowledge structures in adaptive learning environments. *Applied Cognitive Psychology, 20,* 333–342.

Kalyuga, S., Ayres, P., Chandler, P., & Sweller, J. (2003). The expertise reversal effect. Educational Psychologist, 38, 23–31.

Kalyuga, S., Chandler, P., & Sweller, J. (2004). When redundant on-screen text in multimedia technical instruction can interfere with learning. *Human Factors, 46*(3), 567–581.

Kirkwood, A. & Price, L. (2014). Technology-enhanced learning and teaching in higher education: What is 'enhanced' and how do we know? A critical literature review. *Learning, Media and Technology, 39*(1) pp. 6–36.

Kirkwood, A. (2009). E-learning: You don't always get what you hope for. Technology, Pedagogy and Proceedings, ascilite Sydney, 2010: Concise: Price & Kirkwood 781 Education, *18*(2), 107–121

Koehler, M. J., & Mishra, P. (2005). What happens when teachers design educational technology? The development of Technological Pedagogical Content Knowledge. *Journal of Educational Computing Research, 32*(2), 131–152.

Koehler, M. J., & Mishra, P. (2009). What is technological pedagogical content knowledge? *Contemporary Issues in Technology and Teacher Education, 9*(1), 60–70.

Lave, J., & Wenger, E. (1991). *Situated learning: Legitimate peripheral participation.* Cambridge: Cambridge University Press.

Lee, E., Brown, M. N., Luft, J. A., & Roehrig, G. H. (2007). Assessing beginning secondary science teachers' PCK: Pilot year results. *School Science and Mathematics, 107*(2), 52–60.

Leh, A. S. (2005). Lessons learned from service learning and reverse mentoring in faculty development: A case study in technology training. *Journal of Technology and Teacher Education, 13*(1), 25–41.

Linnenbrink, E. A., & Pintrich, P. R. (2003). The role of self-efficacy beliefs in student engagement and learning in the classroom. *Reading & Writing Quarterly, 19*(2), 119–137.

Magnusson, S., Krajcik, J., & Borko, H. (1999). Nature, sources, and development of pedagogical content knowledge for science teaching. In J. Gess-Newsome & N. Lederman (Eds.), PCK and Science Education (pp. 95–132). New York, NY: Kluwer Academic Publishers.

Martinez, M., & Schilling, S. (2010). Using technology to engage and educate youth. *New Directions for Youth Development* (127), 51–61. doi:10.1002/yd.362

Mishra, P., & Koehler, M.J. (2006). Technological pedagogical content knowledge: A framework for integrating technology in teacher knowledge. *Teachers College Record, 108*(6), 1017–1054.

Mouza, C. (2008). Learning with laptops: Implementation and outcomes in an urban, under-privileged school. *Journal of Research on Technology in Education, 40*(4), 447–472.

National Council of Teachers of Mathematics. (2000). Principles and standards for school mathematics. Reston, VA: Author.

National Research Council. (2007). Taking science to school: Learning and teaching science in grades K–8. Washington, DC: The National Academies Press.

NEA Education Policy Brief (2008). Closing the gap through extended learning opportunities. [PDF file]. Retrieved from www.nea.org/assets/docs/HE/mf_PB04_ExtendedLearning.pdf

Niess, M. L. (2005). Preparing teachers to teach science and mathematics with technology: Developing a technology pedagogical content knowledge. *Teaching and Teacher Education, 21*, 509–523.

Nelson Laird, T.F., & Kuh, G.D. (2005). Student experiences with information technology and their relationship to other aspects of student engagement. *Research in Higher Education, 46*(2), 211–233.

NCSS. (2016). Powerful and purposeful teaching and learning in elementary school social studies. Retrieved from www.socialstudies.org/positions/powerfulandpurposeful

November, A. (2015). Clearing the confusion between technology rich and innovative poor: Six questions. Novemberlearning.com. Retrieved from http://novemberlearning.com/assets/ClearingtheConfusionbetweenTechnologyRichandInnovativePoorSixQuestions.pdf

Okojie, M. C. P. O., Olinzock, A. A., & Okojie-Boulder, T. C. (2006). The pedagogy of technology integration. *Journal of Technology Studies, 32*(2), 66–71.

Oppenheimer, T. (2003). *The flickering mind: The false promise of technology in the classroom and how learning can be saved.* New York: Random House.

Penuel, W. (2006). Implementation and effects of one-to-one computing initiatives: A research synthesis. *Journal of Research on Technology in Education, 38*(3), 329–348.

Piaget, J. (2013). *The construction of reality in the child* (Vol. 82). Routledge.

Pike. G.R., Kuh, G.D., & McCormick, A.C. (November 2008). Learning community participation and educational outcomes: Direct, indirect, and contingent relationships. Paper presented at the annual meeting of the Association for the Study of Higher Education. Jacksonville, FL.

Price, L., Kirkwood, A. (2010). Technology enhanced learning: Where's the evidence? Proceedings, ascilite Sydney, 2010: Concise: Price & Kirkwood, 772. Retrieved from https://pdfs.semanticscholar.org/b181/f034f48dc0f0d8b607ec1a8d33d8d7a06c23.pdf

Prince, M. (2004). Does active learning work? A review of the research. *Journal of Engineering Education, 93*(3), 223–231.

Project Tomorrow. (2016). *From print to pixel: The role of videos, games, animations and simulations within K–12 education.* Retrieved from www.tomorrow.org/speakup/SU15AnnualReport.html

Project Tomorrow Speak Up Survey. (June 2013. "From Chalkboard to Tablets: The Emergence of the K–12 Digital Learner" p. 12.

Rias, M. R. & Zaman, H. B. (2013). Understanding the role of prior knowledge in a multimedia learning application. *Australasian Journal of Education Technology, 29*(4) 537–548.

Richardson, V., & Placier, P. (2001). Teacher change. In V. Richardson (Ed.), Handbook of research on teaching (4th ed., pp. 905–947). Washington: American Educational Research Association.

Roblyer, M. D. (2005). Educational technology research that makes a difference: Series introduction. *Contemporary Issues in Technology and Teacher Education, 5*(2), 192–201.

Roblyer, M. D., & Knezek, G. A. (2003). New millenium research for educational technology: A call for a national research agenda. *Journal of Research on Technology in Education, 36*(1), 60–71.

Roschelle, J., Pea, R., Hoadley, C., Gordin, D. & Means, B. (2000). Changing how and what children learn in school with computer-based technologies. *The Future of Children: Children and Computer Technology, 10*(2), 76–101.

Rule, A. (2006). The components of authentic learning. *Journal of Authentic Learning, 3*(1) 1–10.

Schackow, T. E., Chavez, M., Loya, L., & Friedman, M.. (2004). Audience response system: Effect on learning in family medicine residents. *Family Medicine, 36*(7): 496–504.

Shulman, L. S. (1986). Those who understand: Knowledge growth in teaching. *Educational Researcher, 15*(2), 4–14.

Spires, H., Lee, J., Turner, K., & Johnson, J. (2008). Having our say: Middle grade student perspectives on school, technologies, and academic engagement. *Journal of Research on Technology in Education, 40*(4), 497–515. Retrieved from www.unc.edu/world/

Swanson, C.B. (2006). Tracking U.S. trends. The Information Edge: Using Data to Accelerate Achievement. *Education Week, 25*(35), 50–53.

Vaala, S., Ly, A., & Levine, M. (2015). Getting a read on the app stores: A market scan and analysis of children's literacy apps. Joan Ganz Cooney Center. Retrieved from www.joanganzcooneycenter.org/wp-content/uploads/2015/12/jgcc_gettingaread.pdf

Vygotsky, L.S. (1978) *Mind in society: The development of higher psychological processes.* London: Harvard University Press.

Wartella, E. (2015). Educational apps: What we do and do not know. *Psychological Science in the Public Interest, 16*(1), 1–2.

Wenglinsky, H. (1998). Does it compute? The relationship between educational technology and student achievement in mathematics: A policy information report. Princeton, NJ: Educational Testing Service.

Wenglinsky, H. (2005/2006). Technology and achievement: The bottom line. *Educational Leadership, 63*(4), 29–32.

Index